D0436111

"The story of Starbucks is itself an astonishing read. But what's even better is getting a true insider's view of how it all happened. Behar was not only there, he was a major force behind the values, programs, systems, and rigor required to build this truly great company. This book is a must-have for any leader who aspires to build an enduringly great company."

—Keith Yamashita, chairman, Stone Yamashita Partners

"*It's Not About the Coffee* is a testament to Behar's profound grasp of the link between relationships—let's call it human connectivity—and success. The principles in this book, when taken to heart, will resolve issues of customer loyalty and employee engagement. Read it!"

—Susan Scott, author of *Fierce Conversations*

"It's wonderful, after years of listening to Howard think out loud, to see his focus on humanity in business captured so clearly. Howard's ten basic principles illustrate how genuine, purposeful, and caring attention to your people can drive extraordinary results."

—Craig E. Weatherup, former president of PepsiCo and chairman and CEO of Pepsi-Cola

"When Howard speaks of words like *mission, pride,* and *service,* he is laying out the tenets for running a business and building one of the greatest brands in the world. The by-product of his strategy is a corporate culture that stems from individuals who are inspired and empowered to work for the greater good of the brand and its customers. This book is a step-by-step guide for people searching for daily inspiration and those meant to deliver it."

—Kevin Plank, CEO, Under Armour

"Howard stands alone as a person who lives his deepest principles in the workplace and inspires others to do so. Through his example, success, and concrete insights, *It's Not About the Coffee* has the potential to be life changing for executives who want to inspire genuine greatness in their teams and bring more meaning to their own lives. This book has never left my bedside table."

—Chip Adams, partner, Rosewood Capital

It's Not About the Coffee

PORTFOLIO

It's Not About the Coffee

Leadership Principles from a Life at Starbucks

HOWARD BEHAR
WITH JANET GOLDSTEIN

Portfolio

PORTFOLIO
Published by the Penguin Group
Penguin Group (USA) Inc., 375 Hudson Street,
New York, New York 10014, U.S.A.
Penguin Group (Canada), 90 Eglinton Avenue East, Suite 700, Toronto,
Ontario, Canada M4P 2Y3 (a division of Pearson Penguin Canada Inc.)
Penguin Books Ltd, 80 Strand, London WC2R 0RL, England
Penguin Ireland, 25 St. Stephen's Green, Dublin 2, Ireland
(a division of Penguin Books Ltd)
Penguin Books Australia Ltd, 250 Camberwell Road, Camberwell,
Victoria 3124, Australia (a division of Pearson Australia Group Pty Ltd)
Penguin Books India Pvt Ltd, 11 Community Centre,
Panchsheel Park, New Delhi–110 017, India
Penguin Group (NZ), 67 Apollo Drive, Rosedale, North Shore 0632,
New Zealand (a division of Pearson New Zealand Ltd)
Penguin Books (South Africa) (Pty) Ltd, 24 Sturdee Avenue,
Rosebank, Johannesburg 2196, South Africa

Penguin Books Ltd, Registered Offices: 80 Strand, London WC2R 0RL, England

First published in 2007 by Portfolio, a member of Penguin Group (USA) Inc.

1 3 5 7 9 10 8 6 4 2

Grateful acknowledgment is made for permission to reprint excerpts from the following
works:
    "To be of use" from *Circles on the Water* by Marge Piercy. Copyright © 1982 by Marge
Piercy. Used by permission of Alfred A. Knopf, a division of Random House, Inc.
    "Please Hear What I'm Not Saying" by Charles C. Finn. Used by permission of the
author. www.poetrybycharlescfinn.com

LIBRARY OF CONGRESS CATALOGING IN PUBLICATION DATA
Behar, Howard.
It's not about the coffee: leadership lessons from a life at Starbucks / Howard Behar
p. cm.
Includes bibliographical references and index.
ISBN 978-1-59184-192-0
1. Leadership—Psychological aspects. 2. Integrity. 3. Customer relations.
4. Behar, Howard. 5. Starbucks Coffee Company. I. Title.
II. Title: Leadership lessons from a life at Starbucks.
HD57.7.B444 2007
658.4'092—dd22   2007029129

Printed in the United States of America   Set in Granjon
Designed by BTD/NYC

TO

Lynn,

Sarina and Michael, Scott and Kim,

and our four wonderful grandchildren,

Sydney, Ella, Matthew, and Zoey,

who make it easy to

say yes all the time.

The work of the world is common as mud.
Botched, it smears the hands, crumbles to dust.
But the thing worth doing well done
has a shape that satisfies, clean and evident.
Greek amphoras for wine or oil,
Hopi vases that held corn, are put in museums
but you know they were made to be used.
The pitcher cries for water to carry
and a person for work that is real.

—FROM MARGE PIERCY'S
"TO BE OF USE"

Contents

FOREWORD by Howard Schultz   XV

INTRODUCTION: *It's About the People—All the People*   1

1. KNOW WHO YOU ARE: *Wear One Hat*   11

2. KNOW WHY YOU'RE HERE: *Do It Because It's Right, Not Because It's Right for Your Résumé*   29

3. THINK INDEPENDENTLY: *The Person Who Sweeps the Floor Should Choose the Broom*   49

4. BUILD TRUST: *Care, Like You Really Mean It*   65

5. LISTEN FOR THE TRUTH: *The Walls Talk*   79

6. BE ACCOUNTABLE: *Only the Truth Sounds Like the Truth*   99

7. TAKE ACTION: *Think Like a Person of Action, and Act Like a Person of Thought*   113

Contents

8. FACE CHALLENGE: *We Are Human Beings First* 127

9. PRACTICE LEADERSHIP: *The Big Noise and the Still, Small Voice* 139

10. DARE TO DREAM: *Say Yes, the Most Powerful Word in the World* 157

ACKNOWLEDGMENTS 167

ENDNOTES 171

INDEX 175

A Note to Readers

lthough this book is titled *It's Not About the Coffee,* of course it *is* about the coffee—it's about the people and the coffee. Without the people who buy, roast, deliver, prepare, and serve the coffee, we wouldn't have Starbucks. It is the true essence of Starbucks that there can be no coffee without people.

In the same vein, although this book *is* about principles of leadership from my life at Starbucks, you won't find these lessons in any official Starbucks guide to leadership success. The fact is, there isn't a recipe for success at Starbucks, and there is no one official guide to leadership techniques or beliefs. Each person must find an individual way to contribute to the organization and the people we serve. There have been many books and articles written about Starbucks, each with their own point of view. This book is based on my own personal path— the lessons I discovered, practiced, and taught before and during my leadership at Starbucks. These principles and experiences can hopefully, humbly, help you find your own path to success and fulfillment.

Foreword

I am proud and honored to be writing this foreword to Howard Behar's book on the leadership principles he lived and practiced during his life at Starbucks. Howard is the most no-nonsense, no putting on of airs, no fanfare, authentic person you could ever meet. He is all about the truth—whatever it might be. He has an intense style that quickly cuts through the layers that are not relevant. He's also highly passionate and emotional; he wears his feelings on his sleeve. You always know where he stands and where you stand, which is shoulder to shoulder, no matter the personal or organizational challenge.

In terms of leadership, he's the real deal—a natural leader with the skill set to be better than most number ones at many, many companies. But he made the fortuitous choice for me, for Starbucks, and I believe for himself, to join us in 1989 when we were a small regional company. From Howard Behar's first days at the company, he has always stood for and reminded us that "we're in the people business serving coffee, not the coffee business serving people."

This inspiring and practical guidebook, *It's Not About the Coffee,* is about people, and the importance of putting people first. It's about the role that we all play in creating the culture of a company, which brings it to life and sustains its development and direction.

At Starbucks, Howard has always demonstrated that a great business is a business with a conscience. And he has shown in leadership roles spanning more than thirty years that one can do well by doing good. I became a much stronger leader because of his partnership and coaching. I also know that it wasn't just his experience but also his enormous friendship and love of what we were doing that allowed him to have such a profound impact on me, our people, and all the people we serve.

Looking back at the history and success of Starbucks, one thing you'll notice is that we have had great timing. For one thing, we always seem to be able to attract the right person at the right time for the right job. If Howard Behar, along with Orin Smith, did not arrive at the time they did, the company as it exists today would be quite different. I'm quite sure we would not be as resourceful. We'd certainly lack that special chemistry the three of us developed, the almost nonverbal level of understanding that drove so much of what we wanted to do and how we wanted to do it.

To understand the dynamic between us, I think you have to start with the fact that I want to dream big dreams and dream bigger while Howard wants to dream big dreams but then take five steps back to see what could go wrong (even if it's an idea he's championing and passionately wants to turn into a reality). That dynamic, with all its creative conflicts, created a better footprint, a better blueprint for the company because we had the optimism as well as the caution. We never went too fast around the curve. The company had the benefit of differing points of view, but we were always heading in the same direction. There was never an argument about where were going, just how we were going to get there.

Orin provided the balance between the different pathways, plus the financial direction and know-how we needed. Despite the fact that I was the formal head of the company, we organized it in a way where there was tremendous respect for one another and never any divide and conquer. We bonded to form an entity which many in the company appropriately called H2O (for Howard, Howard, and Orin). We became an essential ingredient, like water is for coffee.

Between Howard and me, the language we spoke was one of trust. There was a mutual awareness of the sacrifices it takes to build an organization that few people understand. As a leader, you're always trying to build confidence, so the vulnerability and doubt you experience aren't characteristics that a lot of us feel comfortable revealing and it can be very lonely. Howard and I had each other to talk to. Our conversations were about strategy, but they were also structured around our own dynamics. The results that followed came out of those conversations.

And Howard could make things happen like no one else. One of the stories we don't talk about that often is how we almost lost the company in late 1989. We went to Chicago to show potential investors that the Starbucks concept wasn't a local phenomenon. But we were failing just as we were trying to raise more money. Howard said to me, "I will move to Chicago and I will not leave until we've gotten it right." He knew the people there needed to believe in what they were doing, to understand that the cause was bigger than their individual role or store, and to know that their endeavors mattered.

Through his action of moving to Chicago, he showed the caring and team-building he's famous for and he demonstrated the principles of this book. His ability to pull people in, combined with his total commitment to our goals, elevated the mood through the entire company and strongly affected our performance.

His relentless belief in our cause, in walking our talk, in honoring the truth, meant that he always had *all* the people in mind, whatever the issue at hand. He taught us how to listen to all the people we served. He helped us put our values into action.

Howard understands the importance of embracing the human condition and respecting people for who they are. People want to be around him because he makes them feel better about themselves. He provides a formula for people to succeed. If you follow just some of the principles in this book, you will be a wiser, more effective, and more successful human being and leader.

I believe that this book is a must-read for:

- each and every entrepreneur and small business owner. The early stage is the most important time in the life of any business. It is the time when the culture and values are imprinted in the business.
- anyone who is at an early stage or growth period in their own career and wants to understand what it means to dream big dreams. This book can help you identify and develop your own values, skills, and goals and make sure they guide your life and career.

- any individual or team member who wants to understand the value of human behavior and who wants to elevate the morale and results inside their own group or organization.
- any business leader who is struggling with their existing culture or value proposition, this is a great book to remind you of what is possible.
- for any organization, not only a business, looking for a good resource on how to manage people and how to build things that endure.

Howard, and this book, offer a simple set of concrete principles that can guide the leadership actions you take in your own life. *It's Not About the Coffee* is a call to create lives, workplaces, and a world that we can be proud of. There is no better teacher than Howard Behar.

—HOWARD SCHULTZ

It's Not About the Coffee

Introduction

It's About the People—
All the People

Never doubt that a small group of thoughtful,
committed citizens can change the world.
— MARGARET MEAD

We're all human" is the mantra that says it all to me. None of us are really customers, or employees, or managers, or bosses. We're people. We're human beings.

At Starbucks we're in the human service business, not the customer service business. That means the coffee has to be excellent, from the sourcing and growing to the roasting and brewing. The vision has to be inspiring and meaningful to our partners, the communities we're a part of, and all the people we serve. Our finances have to be in order so we can do the work we love. But without people, we have nothing. With people, we have something even bigger than coffee.

If you grow people, the people grow the business. That's it. That's the number-one priority. If your people are better human beings, they'll be better partners of the company. If you think of your customers as people, you'll make a connection with them, and they'll come back over and over again to enjoy the coffee and the experience. If you contribute meaningfully to the world around you, that caring comes back to you in kind.

My whole life, I've been driven to learn, grow, and lead. As a child I was a dreamer. I was motivated to accomplish things. Whether it was sweeping my family's grocery store, or learning the furniture business from the ground up in my brother and brother-in-law's store, or finding the best person in the furniture business to work for when I was ready for bigger challenges.

I discovered there were always people to teach me things. Out of a combination of necessity and desire, I became a student of myself and other people. I practiced what I learned—from the power of goal-setting and self-knowledge to the importance of building trust and speaking the truth. And of course I learned about successes and failures and how to handle them. And boy, did I learn from my mistakes—over and over again. I learned what worked and what didn't for me and for others. And I'm still learning.

In fact, it was only after failing at a business that I loved that I got the chance to put the leadership principles I had learned to work in an organization. At the time, my passion and ability to motivate people and build a sense of community hadn't been enough to overcome the culture of a new management and their overriding drive to boost profits at the expense of their people. I searched for a place where I'd flourish.

As it so happened, I often found myself sitting in the Bellevue Starbucks, just outside of Seattle, pondering my next move. But always a retailer at heart, as I sat there planning a possible new retail venture, I was making mental notes about the Starbucks store I was sitting in—*Don't get too slick. Good texture. Need more chairs.*

Just as I was about to finalize the papers to start my own business, a goal I had pursued and delayed several times, the stars aligned, and I signed on at Starbucks, in 1989, at the age of forty-four. My dreams and the Starbucks dream turned out to be a match made in heaven. We lived, breathed, and taught the principles of a people-centered organization. We put our philosophy into action and to the test every day.

As my path became clearer and as our drive to create a people-centered organization took hold, I worked more intensely to share what I knew with the people I worked with and lived alongside every day. I cajoled, pushed, confronted, and cared. I reached out beyond the office and conference rooms with phone calls and visits to stores. I spoke at gatherings large and small to share what I learned and to inspire others.

Wherever I am, I still visit as many Starbucks stores as I can each week. I've discovered that my hunger for wisdom about the human dimensions of leadership and building a successful organization has only grown throughout the years and has reached far beyond the walls of Starbucks.

I also know from firsthand experience that there's a large gap between the wisdom of knowing what's right and the wisdom to do what's right. The principles I've learned and taught sound simple because they are based on basic human truths. But putting them into practice is hard because it is human nature to avoid the truth, both with ourselves and with others.

Your part is to discover *your* truth. When you do so, you tap into your passion, unexplored strengths, and individual gaps so you can grow, lead, and achieve your goals and find your potential for personal and organizational success.

Ten Principles of Personal Leadership

At Starbucks there's a little green booklet, called *The Green Apron Book,* which sets down the guiding principles for all the people who work at the company.

It's a simple book, barely a booklet, but no one ever complains about its simplicity. The guidelines are merely reminders of what we stand for in our Starbucks stores—what we *can* do, not what we must or can't do.

As we grew from a small to a much larger group of committed individuals, *The Green Apron Book* was a way to capture and write down the things that mattered to us about our mission and the kind of company we were creating. In the same spirit, the principles of personal leadership I've learned and taught and present in this book are principles that *everyone* can embrace. I've used them as touchstones to keep me honest and to keep me clear.

They've also withstood the test kitchen of my leadership at Starbucks. The principles are literally brewed into the way we work, make decisions, confront problems, care about one another, persevere, and create opportunities for our future. This book, these principles, are trusted markers that can set your course in the turbulent sea of business, commerce, and life.

I've used these principles as I've coached hundreds of leaders at every level. Not every principle will be equally meaningful to you or equally challenging for you to remember and practice. But I can guarantee you that you won't go wrong if you use these ten principles as a guiding force in leading yourself and, if it's your goal, in leading others.

1. KNOW WHO YOU ARE: *Wear One Hat*

Our success is directly related to our clarity and honesty about who we are, who we're *not,* where we want to go, and how we're going to get there. When organizations are clear about their values, purpose, and goals, they find the energy and passion to do great things.

2. KNOW WHY YOU'RE HERE: *Do It Because It's Right, Not Because It's Right for Your Résumé*

The path to success comes from doing things for the right reasons. You can't succeed if you don't know what you're trying to accomplish and without everyone being aligned with the goal. Look for purpose and passion in yourself and the people you lead. If they're not there, do something.

3. THINK INDEPENDENTLY: *The Person Who Sweeps the Floor Should Choose the Broom*

People are not "assets," they are human beings who have the capacity to achieve results beyond what is thought possible. We need to get rid of rules—real and imagined—and encourage the independent thinking of others and ourselves.

4. BUILD TRUST: *Care, Like You Really Mean It*

Caring is not a sign of weakness but rather a sign of strength, and it can't be faked—within an organization, with the people we serve, or in our local or global communities. Without trust and caring, we'll never know what could have been possible. Without freedom from fear, we can't dream, and we can't reach our potential.

5. LISTEN FOR THE TRUTH: *The Walls Talk*

Put the time into listening, even to what's not said, and amazing results will follow. You'll know what your customers want, you'll know why the passion is missing from your organization, and you'll learn solutions to problems that have been sitting there waiting to be picked.

6. BE ACCOUNTABLE: *Only the Truth Sounds Like the Truth*

No secrets, no lies of omission, no hedging and dodging. Take responsibility and say what needs to be said, with care and respect.

7. TAKE ACTION: *Think Like a Person of Action, and Act Like a Person of Thought*

Find the sweet spot of passion, purpose, and persistence. "It's all about the people" isn't an idea, it's an action. Feel, do, think. Find the balance, but act.

8. FACE CHALLENGE: *We Are Human Beings First*

Use all the principles to guide you during the hardest times. If the challenge is too big, if you find yourself stuck, take smaller bites. But remember to put people first, and you'll find the guidance you need.

9. PRACTICE LEADERSHIP: *The Big Noise and the Still, Small Voice*

Leading can be the noisy "I'm here!" kind of thing. But don't ever forget that leaders are just ordinary human beings. Don't let the noise crowd out the truth. Listen to your still, small voice. Let quiet be your guide.

10. DARE TO DREAM: *Say Yes, the Most Powerful Word in the World*

Big dreams mean big goals, big hopes, big joys. Say yes, and enjoy all that you are doing, and help others to do the same.

Valuable Reminders

As people who traveled through my office over the years know, my way of reminding myself about this journey of true self and purpose was to put words of wisdom, which I used as guard-rails for my journey, on my walls.

When I heard a piece of advice, read something that struck me as a blinding flash of insight, I wrote it down, used it as a reference point, and quoted its lessons as I taught and mentored others. These weren't quotes that became slogans in company hallways and restrooms. These were sometimes direct and sometimes enigmatic words of wisdom that became a launching pad for many positive and difficult conversations I had with people and became part of the institutional memory for the people who make up the culture of Starbucks.

Over time, I framed and hung many of these quotes, and other people began to add to what is now an extensive collection of black frames by giving me quotes that are important to them or, they think, relevant to me.

This collection is really a map of my life. The quotes represent my education. I learned from the wisdom of the ages, from mentors, and from experiences. Making these lessons permanent and putting them where I could see them every day reinforced what was important to me. It's not so different from going to a church or a mosque or a temple—we need to be reminded of what is important, of the lessons we've learned, and of the things that guide how we work and how we live our lives.

The lessons—and the difficult, joyful, challenging, emotional conversations often begun in my office beneath the frames—have been remembered, embraced, and passed on by Starbucks people around the globe.

It's my belief that we need these lessons more than ever, and they need to be shared as widely as possible. The time has passed when leaders and followers, bosses and employees, have distinct roles with distinct requirements. We are all people. We're all human beings.

As work becomes less hierarchical, as our world economy becomes more and more about relationships and connecting, I believe the principles of personal leadership are more important than ever. Although leading others is an honor, it begins with an obligation.

It brings an obligation, first, to continually develop your self and, second, to help develop leaders—not only leaders with a capital *L*, those with official titles and organizational responsibilities, but also leaders with a small *l*, who are all of us. We're all responsible for leading ourselves to realize our potential and to make the greatest possible contribution to work and the world around us.

However, here's the irony—and an invitation. At its most basic, "It's all about the people" has always meant it's *not* about *me*. It's about *us* and what we can do together. These principles and this book are about you and us, all of us in the game of work and life. What you can do in your job, your career, your life, what we can all do together is more than most of us can imagine. If we know who we are, know where we're going, and go there with a spirit of human service, the entire journey becomes far less daunting and far more fulfilling.

1. KNOW WHO YOU ARE

Wear One Hat

Seek out that particular mental attitude which makes
you feel most deeply and vitally alive. . . .
—WILLIAM JAMES

Wearing one hat is the epitome of personal leadership. It is the starting point—and the end point—of the lifelong process of discovering who you are and what you stand for. When you wear one hat:

- You know what makes you feel most deeply alive.
- You feel good about yourself.
- You have no need for secrets or pretending or posturing.
- You can lead yourself and others from a place of clarity and integrity.

When you wear one hat, you prioritize who you are and refuse to be anything less. You value yourself and the work you do. When something isn't right, including your work, you know that, too. When you know who you are, everything else becomes easier—even the hard stuff.

We all have too many hats in our closets, whether they're Starbucks hats or baseball caps or hats with logos from every trade show and sales meeting we've ever been to. And it's common to hear people complain about wearing too many hats.

Being busy and juggling lots of different roles can make us edgy, inefficient, frustrated, and hard to be around. The start-up entrepreneur who is secretary, CFO, marketing director, and president can be overloaded and overextended. But if all those hats are all serving the same goals and values, the person can gain the skills and find the support needed to grow the enterprise.

Edward de Bono, in *Six Hat Thinking*, discussed the different ways that we think, and he labeled them *hats* to eliminate any sense of hierarchy or judgmentalism. The white hat stands for neutral and objective thinking, the black hat for the devil's advocate, and the green hat for fertile, creative thinking. His point was that using symbolic hats to signal different perspectives helps groups and individuals create honest dialogue.

The one hat I'm talking about, which has been so powerful in my life and for the people I've worked with, is the hat that helps us to find and stay true to a deeper sense of ourselves and our values. Our personal hat, our one hat, is a metaphor for being consistent with oneself. What you see is what you get. One-hat leadership, like one-hat living, is synonymous with honesty, clarity, passion, and a sense of being truly engaged and alive.

> **People who feel good about themselves produce good results.**
>
> — KENNETH H. BLANCHARD AND SPENCER JOHNSON,
> *The One Minute Manager*

In *The One Minute Manager*, that deceptively simple leadership primer, Ken Blanchard and Spencer Johnson say it as plainly as I've seen it: "People who feel good about themselves produce good results." That's it. Our success is directly related to our clarity and honesty about who we are, where we want to go, and how we're going to get there.

The same can be said for organizations. Organizations are just aggregations of people. An organization that wears one hat knows what it stands for and has the energy and clarity of purpose to succeed. There are no secrets, no hiding, no pretending, just the honest drive to fulfill the organization's dreams and goals and to fulfill the dreams and goals of its people.

Whose Hat Are You Wearing?

When I was in my twenties, I moved into my first real executive-level job. In this new role, I ran a chain of twenty or so furniture stores based in Portland, Oregon. It was the seventies, the city was growing rapidly, and the job was new and exciting. I was married, with a baby, and I was eager to succeed. I started to think I might actually have a career at something—not just work I was good at but a future building a company in a business I loved.

I threw myself into the job. I was passionate about everything—the merchandise, the displays, the customers, and the salespeople on the floor. I wanted to be the best, to serve the best, to deliver the best. I was emotionally involved, and I said what I really thought. My passion showed in everything I did. I was highly motivated and focused, and just plain excited to make things happen. But I guess it was too much passion. One day, the CEO and chairman caught me totally by surprise as we were about to get on the elevator. He said, "Howard, you just can't go around wearing your feelings on your sleeve!"

When I heard that criticism, it was as if I had been totally rejected. Something inside me shifted. I hadn't realized that by expressing my true feelings about the work we were doing and how I wanted things to be, I was behaving in a way that made other people uncomfortable. I was embarrassed, self-conscious, and worried. I began to modulate, to moderate my feelings. I started sitting on the "hands" of my emotions. I tried to limit them and squeeze them into a little, tiny place within me to project a more stoic, subdued, "professional" image.

Being "professional" was damn hard, but I came up with a plan that I thought would work. Every time I needed to behave in a certain way to please someone else, I would imagine myself putting on a different hat. There was one hat for work. There was one hat for my wife. There was another hat for my daughter and still another one for my friends. I learned to present a different person depending on the circumstance I was in, in an attempt to keep my emotions in check.

For the most part, my technique worked, but I was a nervous wreck. I was trying to be too many things to too many people. I developed a nervous habit of bending and unbending paper clips, dozens a day, which morphed into tearing up bits of paper—thinking that paper clips were too expensive too waste.

Finally, a friend I respected said to me, "What are you doing? Who are you trying to be? What happened to Howard?" He showed me that by faking it—by changing myself to meet the expectations of others—I was preventing myself from doing what I did best. Sitting on my hands had me sitting on my ideals and goals. I was too busy juggling a load of different hats. When I stifled my emotional reactions, I stifled my passion as well. Trying to act the "right" way, I cut off pieces of myself. I needed to learn how to bring my emotions to work so they could work for me and could inspire others.

From that point on, I worked hard to do one thing—find and wear just one hat, my hat. Not someone else's idea of fashion but a hat that just plain fit. Remarkably, finding my one hat meant that every success and every mistake that shaped and informed the way I looked at business and life was wrapped around one true and authentic self. When I began being honest with myself and others, honest with my thoughts and my feelings, it set me on my journey to know myself and discover my true passion. I committed to finding my one self and my purpose, and to living that self every day so no one had to ask, "What happened to Howard?" I decided to lead, not by trying to be a leader, but by trying to live in a way that was more true to me as a human being.

If you spend more time pretending to be someone you think you're supposed to be than you spend being yourself, you might be wearing too many hats. This is a hard thing to realize. Most of us think we have to juggle many different hats for different roles in order to be successful. We think the different roles in our lives demand that we act as if we're different people. But at what cost? If you wake up in the morning, look across the bed and say, "I have to put on my spouse or partner hat," you're either in the wrong bed or someone has to make some adjustments.

You have to remember that you have choices. It might take changing your attitude, changing companies, or even changing careers, but you owe it to yourself to find the one hat that you can wear every day in every area of your life.

Know What Really Matters to You

In the retail business you learn about human nature. In the furniture business you learn about the intimate parts of people's lives—their tastes and conflicts, their finances, their dreams and aspirations.

I loved what I did and never really questioned it . . . until an offer came my way to be part of a team that was building an exciting new business of memberships in beautiful outdoor resorts. My mentor wanted me to join him in the new venture he was running. The company's mission captured my imagination. The position would mean more money, more responsibility, and a new challenge, but I wondered if it was right for me.

I had spent my whole career up to that point wanting to be the best I could be in the furniture business. For twenty years I thought of furniture as my life and calling. It might seem odd to be so invested in something so practical. But it was true. That's when my future boss asked me a question that has become part of the story of my life. The question he asked was, "What do you love? Furniture or people?" It wasn't an easy question to answer.

On the one hand, furniture is furniture. But it was also the way I expressed my creativity. Furniture was my art. But when I thought more about it, I realized that the emotions and passion I felt about my work didn't have to do with the furniture, they had to do with the people. I didn't love furniture. I loved the selection and the selling and the whole idea of helping people realize their dreams for their homes and lives. It was my music, just as coffee is for those of us who've made our home at Starbucks. But it was people that I loved—the interaction among people, serving other people, learning from other people.

I took the opportunity. My one hat was the same, but now it had a name—serving people—and it gave me a new view of where I was headed and what I might achieve.

Goals Give Us Tools to Put Dreams into Action

If each of us is on a lifelong journey to find our hat, to know who we are, then by implication we are all on a journey to somewhere. I believe that our passion for that destination is what makes us engaged and purposeful about our work and lives. Without a dream, without goals, we have no direction. As the old expression says, "If you don't know where you're going, any path will get you there."

William James, the visionary turn-of-the-century psychologist and philosopher, might be considered one of the fathers of self-actualization. He understood the power of our thoughts to affect our lives. His advice then is as true today as ever: "Seek out that particular mental attitude which makes you feel most deeply and vitally alive, along with which comes the inner voice which says, 'This is the real me,' and when you have found that attitude, follow it."

Many, many people are afraid to follow their dreams. They are afraid of goals or at least resist them. They think goals take the fluidity and spontaneity out of life. And they worry about how they'll feel if they don't reach them. But we need to remember that goals are not a blueprint; they simply provide a vision.

Think about it in terms of a fishing line. A big goal, like a big fish, puts some tension on the line. You've got to have tension to succeed. You can't catch a fish without it. If your line goes slack, you know you've lost a big one. If you yank too hard, you risk losing the fish and the lure as well.

We begin teaching our children values at an early age. We offer gentle but continuous pressure to gradually pull and lure them into mature, thoughtful human beings. But if you lose patience and jerk the line too often, your can lose the child. Rarely is speed, or laying down the law, the best solution. Constant dialogue, clarity, trust, soft tension on the line—those are the qualities that lead to the results and relationships we wish for.

In your life you've got to go after your goals and dreams. Of course, for the passion and the persistence to be there, they need to be aligned with your hat. They need to be true to who you are and what you truly want to accomplish. And yes, you will surely lose some. But you can't catch a dream without tension on the line. So be purposeful. Don't be satisfied just dawdling along.

> **To attempt to climb—to achieve—without a firm objective in life is to attain nothing.**
> — MARY ROEBLING

Nurture and Inspire the Human Spirit

The best companies are on a journey to find their one hat and to be true to it, too. At Starbucks, I've always said we're not in the coffee business serving people, we're in the people business serving coffee. We're passionate about the people who make the coffee, the people we serve, the people we partner with, and the communities we're part of. In so many ways, we continue to change, adapt, grow, and experiment, sometimes at a dizzying pace. But we always try to stay true to our hat.

Jim Collins, coauthor of *Built to Last,* was someone who gave us wise counsel and led some of our most powerful learning sessions as we figured out how to articulate and stay true to the essence of Starbucks. In his book he uses a quote by IBM pioneer Thomas Watson Jr. to bring home the message of wearing one hat: "The only sacred cow in an organization should be its basic philosophy of doing business."

At Starbucks, the dream is being part of an organization with a larger purpose. But in the crush of opening stores, developing new drinks, creating new partnerships, and meeting investor expectations, it is easy to forget the dream and to take off our one hat. It takes commitment and discipline to constantly remind ourselves to stay true to our core values and our big dream. We knew that in order to grow, not for two or ten years but for twenty or thirty years into the future, we would need to articulate our hat so we could measure ourselves against it. We needed a guardrail to keep us honest about ourselves and true to our dream.

In 1996, we invited Jim Collins to help us define our own Big Hairy Audacious Goal, or BHAG, like the ones identified with the companies studied in *Built to Last.* We brought together lots of different people from our leadership team, and others, to participate in the process. In 1996, we came up with a BHAG statement, which guides us, anchors us, and inspires us to this day: "To be one of the most well-known and respected organizations in the world known for nurturing and inspiring the human spirit."

It's pretty easy to measure, "one of the most well-known and respected organizations." Lots of researchers and journalists assess those things and document them in articles and in "best companies to work for" lists. Starbucks has rated high on these lists since we went public in 1992, and it means a lot to us to receive this kind of outside recognition. But "known for nurturing and inspiring the human spirit"? How the heck do you measure that? It's not a numerical goal. Some executives might say it's too nebulous or just a dream. But it really is a goal. It's our legacy goal, which is bigger than any of us and certainly will outlast us. We just always need to be moving toward it.

We must always be vigilant about measuring ourselves and the individual performance of top leaders against this goal. How? We ask ourselves, and any organization needs to ask itself, do our actions match our goals? Are the things we do every day matching who we are and who we want to be?

Everybody talks about the success of Starbucks. However, there are plenty of people, myself included, who like to look at what we're *not* successful at, what hasn't worked. We've had eighteen years of consecutive earnings growth. That is something remarkable to learn from and to try to continue. So I say yes, we've done lots of good things, and we've had a lot of luck, too. But those of us who have worked for Starbucks can never forget what brought us to this party. It's not the thousands of stores in close to fifty countries around the world; it's the commitment we've had to one another as human beings that has led to our success as individuals and as an organization.

When someone looks back in twenty years and writes a study of companies who've set these Big Hairy Audacious Goals like ours to "nurture and inspire the human spirit," I'd like to think that when they talk about Starbucks, they'll talk about how we stayed with ours and that we lived it every day.

One-Hat Goals

At a young age, we have many aspirations, interests, drives, and dreams, not one to the exclusion of others. But when we're honest with ourselves, we can begin to recognize our strengths and our passions. We know whether we love the outdoors, the arts, and/or intellectual pursuits. We test out whether we like making things, doing things, and/or thinking things up. We know if we are driven to start a family or create a life with a significant other. We explore whether we seek money, fame, adventure, or security.

When our passions become clear, our strengths and goals come more sharply into focus. What we're good at and what we like to do are often linked. Over a lifetime, we all learn skills, improve, change direction, and work to moderate our flaws. But our natural talents give us the energy we need to persist in achieving the goals and results we seek.

Goals are emotional. If a goal is not working for you, you're not connected to it. Raise it, make it meaningful, make it touch something in you that you want. Or take it off your list.

It's easy to reject the idea of goals at companies because they are so often disconnected from the people who need to make them happen. Too often leaders and bosses don't get buy-in. They don't get input from as many people as they can, and they don't stay with it. When you set out to accomplish something, it's going to require effort. There had better be an emotional connection. There had better be some buy-in. There had better be some understanding of what it means, what it's all about, and why.

I can't tell you how many companies I've been to where I've asked, "OK, I understand that you're trying to sell something, or that you want to open thirty stores, but why? Other than making a living, what are your objectives? What are you trying to do? What do your people want to have happen?" Forget about the budget and annual goals. Think big. Think about the long term. Think about goals that seem like dreams, goals that have so much emotion attached to them that you can almost taste them. They are so much more powerful.

Values Matter—The Path That Takes You There

The foundation of knowing who you are is being aware of your values, your hat. What is really important to you? Knowing your own values and being in a work environment that allows you to be true to them every day are the key to more than just job satisfaction; they are also the key to a happy life.

We all have to make sure we're pursuing what is most important. Don't compromise—don't be less than your true self. None of the principles of personal leadership will hold water if they aren't built on a solid foundation. Caring, independent thinking, listening, and truth telling will not support you and your organization if they are not true to who you are and aligned with the goals of the organization. Sometimes you will have to make hard decisions in order to keep your values intact, but make them. The stakes couldn't be higher.

Ask yourself questions and test your answers. For example:

- What gets you up and excited to the point of anxiety to do the work?
- What are you willing to sacrifice for this job, this role, this dream?
- How competitive are you? How do you treat people? Do you value and practice honesty?
- What rewards satisfy you?
- How important is it that you live near where you grew up? How willing are you to travel?
- How important is independence to you?
- What is your threshold for stress? What brings you into a "flow" state of intense time-stopping engagement?
- Are you most comfortable and excited to work in entrepreneurial and start-up settings or in established "knowable" environments with more secure resources and capital?
- What will you regret not doing or not trying?
- What is the one thing that makes you comfortable being who you are?

Think about where you are on a scale of 1 to 10 for the following traits (1 being lowest, 10 highest):

- Risk orientation
- Working as part of a team
- Independence
- Being in charge, being autonomous
- People-driven (as opposed to project-driven)

There's another topic that is much discussed in the context of values, and that is the notion of balance. In my mind, balance isn't a value. When you wear one hat and live and act based on your values, balance isn't the issue. Yes, you may go through a time with too much work and too much stress. You will surely go through times of crisis and conflict. But when you wear one hat, your life has meaning and passion. Your whole life is engaged in the choices, struggles, and joys you experience.

You're not trying to "balance" your life, you're living it. When you know yourself, when you wear one hat, when you "walk your talk," whether it's at work or at home, you will see yourself learning, growing, and changing. Those are values that you can use to guide your life and lead others.

Values over Money: How Our Hat Guides Us at Starbucks

Sometimes there's a price to pay when we hold on to our values, whether they are our own, our family's, or our organization's. There can be the pain of saying no to exciting opportunities that would take us away from what's most important at a deeper level. And there is also the pain of saying yes and following through on challenging commitments we make to ourselves and one another.

Early on at Starbucks, we quickly figured out that when there was pain—economic pain, conflict, or disappointment over a failed idea—our hat was still our hat, our values were still our values, and sticking with them was the most important thing we could do. We knew if we broke that trust with ourselves and our customers, we wouldn't be who we are; we wouldn't be on the right path.

Part of that trust was grounded in our belief that people mattered and we had to show it in everything we did. For example, we were adamant about raising the pay of the people in our stores above minimum wage. We were fully dedicated to compensating everyone as a true partner, as a valued member of a team, and to reinforcing our belief that everyone, not just high-level managers and executives, had an important contribution to make. It was something that meant a lot to me personally, and it was something that fit with the vision of the kind of organization our founder, Howard Schultz, wanted to build.

It was also consistent with the vision I had signed up to help pursue. Clearly our goal about wages wasn't designed to gain a business advantage. Any retail or food-service expert would tell you that the best thing to do is to try to lower your labor costs. But here we were trying to raise our labor costs intentionally, because we felt it was the right thing to do and believed it was in the best long-term interest of our business.

I took on the task of figuring out how we could make the salary adjustment a reality, knowing that it was going to be tough but that we would do our best to make it happen. Our team did days and days of analysis to prove we could afford the increase. Our research told us it was going to cost about 1 percent of sales, which is a lot, but we felt it was an amount we could absorb. I was thrilled when we put it into effect.

When we finally implemented the new salary structure, the costs turned out to be *double* what we had anticipated—over 2 percent of sales. This was a huge difference and a huge problem that we hadn't planned on.

I had to suck it up and admit that I made a huge mistake on the numbers. Still, we didn't even consider rolling back the wages. Our values mattered more than the money. We didn't feel that any of us could walk down the hallway, look someone in the face, and say, "We're all in this together," if that wasn't the truth. We didn't ignore our value of caring for the people—all the people.

We struggled to make the financial formula work, but in the end, offering our partners fair compensation and benefits has become one of Starbucks's shining successes. Knowing our values—knowing who we were and our dream of who we wanted to become—helped us stick together in our shared purpose of nurturing and inspiring the human spirit.

Wearing One Hat Takes the Wisdom of Others

To know who you are may sound like a solo enterprise, but it's not. Every book you read, person you meet, and experience you have is an opportunity to learn about yourself and what you're made of. We all need the wisdom of others. There's nothing like your own spouse or roommate or child to keep you honest about who you are.

Not only do we need people to question us, we also need to surround ourselves with people who support us, see our potential, and see what we can become. You deserve to spend time with and work with people who value your contributions and can guide them as well.

If you're not reaching your potential, you can make a conscious effort to learn from others and build your skills and self-awareness. This goes for each of us as individuals, leaders, and mentors, and it goes for organizations as well. We need to learn and stretch ourselves, and we need to create teams and organizations that foster learning, risk-taking, and change.

There is nothing more powerful than the journey toward reaching our potential—or even beyond our potential. Max

De Pree, the legendary head of Herman Miller and son of its founder, talks about running ninety-five yards in a hundred-yard dash. If you go all out to run ninety-five yards but don't complete the last five, you've made the first ninety-five yards pointless.

When a panel assembler at a Herman Miller meeting heard this story, he wrote to De Pree to fill in a missing point. The assembler explained that serious runners visualize a 110-yard dash. That way, when you're in a race, no one will overtake you before you reach the finish line. This concept applies to everything we do. It tells us to think beyond the whole, or we may always fall short and undermine our results. We need to think *beyond* our potential to achieve great things. If you shortchange your dreams, if you shortchange your sense of who you are, you'll shortchange your life.

Learning—from experts, workshops, trainings, practical experiments, therapy, coaches, observing, and silence—is *all* good. It's how we test and hone our values, our potential, and our goals in the real world of life.

We Don't Find Opportunity, It Finds Us

Everybody has it in themselves to find opportunities or make opportunities happen. To do so you have to be an optimist, about you. You have to believe in yourself. So—surprise, surprise—it all starts with the journey to know who you are and to find your one hat. The journey isn't easy. Your family background, your upbringing, even your genetic makeup, all can put a weight on your shoulders. But if you're honest with yourself and look for a way, you will find it.

Some say we create our opportunities. I believe opportunities present themselves in mysterious ways, and we can choose to

see them. When you know who you are, you will see a path of
possibility literally unfold before you. You will be gently guided
to follow it, or you'll create your own opportunity. Each life is
filled with possibilities, but most of us miss the magical places to
dig. Keep your eyes open, and you will find the treasure.

EXTRA SHOTS: Know Who You Are

• What do you love to do? What motivates you?

• What dreams do you have? Big dreams. Write them down.

• What's getting in the way of achieving your dreams?

• What's on your list that you don't want to do, or be, anymore?

• Whether you're twenty or eighty, what do you want to be known for? How do you want to be remembered?

• Who around you has valuable lessons to offer? Who is inspiring you to go beyond your potential?

• Where are you putting your passion to work right now?

• What would move you toward your goals right now? Are you doing it? Why not? Could you?

2. KNOW WHY YOU'RE HERE

Do It Because It's Right, Not Because It's Right for Your Résumé

The work exists for the person as much as the person exists for the work.

—ROBERT K. GREENLEAF

The most powerful question I can ask someone is, "Why are you here?" When someone brings their passion to work, and it is aligned with the work of the organization, success is the natural outcome. When we know and value why we're here, we experience success in our day-to-day roles, success in our creative ideas and results, success in handling problems, and even success in weathering those times when success seems to be out of our grasp.

People Don't Work on Work, They Work on Dreams

Too often we focus on the tactics and the techniques to build a business rather than the people who *are* the business. Marketing, branding, quality control, technical innovation, sales offerings, acquisitions, and other business activities often demand all our attention rather than the people whose passion, drive, and purpose are essential to making them happen. People think up, create, and stay committed to each of these endeavors. When we know why we're here as individuals and leaders, when our people know why they're here, a sense of purpose carries us forward, and we can do what needs to be done. People want to work on big ideas that matter to them and make a difference. When they do, they find gold.

On the other hand, when our efforts aren't paying off—when profits are down, morale is low, schedules are missed—the problem is usually bigger than the label we give it, and we forget about the larger goals for our team or organization. We might start cutting staff, or expenses, or training—often core elements of the success we have achieved—in a misguided attempt to get results. Yes, tactical decisions need to be made every day, and increasing productivity can be a very good thing. But tactics aren't a means to fulfill a dream; people are.

Most of the time, when things aren't working, the underlying problem is connected to the people, not just the tactics. They may have lost sight of why they're here and what they are contributing. They may not know, remember, or believe in the goals that have been set, or their efforts may have been overlooked or tamped down. As I like to say, it's easy for people to get tangled in their own underwear. We can try to solve problems and make progress by working on the necessary but small stuff—like getting our feet in the right openings. Sometimes we can get tangled in problems of our own making. Or we can make sure we look up to see who's around us and what they need because that's where the answers are going to come from.

Without vigilance it's easy to start chasing money, job titles, power, or even popularity among an inner circle instead of seeing the big picture of the organization. We expend time, money, and effort taking care of ourselves and our image rather than taking care of others. We get tangled in our underwear, in our individual concerns, individual results, and individual résumés. We lose sight of why we're here and what we're trying to accomplish: meeting the bigger needs of our customers, shareholders, and the local and global communities we serve.

The Power of Alignment

In 2001, I had the opportunity to come out of retirement to take on the interim role of president of Starbucks North America. I had spent six exciting and strenuous years as the founding president of Starbucks International, going from zero stores outside North America to four hundred stores in twelve countries around the world in cities from Tokyo to Dubai.

After years of travel and a commitment to my wife, Lynn, that I would take some time off, I retired from day-to-day operations, and we started to unwind. Yet when the call came, I didn't hesitate. I was ready to dive into a new challenge. Plus, Starbucks is family, and you never say no to family.

Unexpectedly, coming back was a jolt. Not the work. Not the energy I needed to get back in the game. Rather it was the feeling I got. There was a problem, a malaise, that I couldn't quite put my finger on. Good work was being done, but it wasn't a happy place.

I've learned that if you ask questions, you get answers. I started talking to people all over the organization. I asked them what they liked and what they didn't. I asked straight out, "If you had a magic wand, what would you change?"

The bottom line was that people felt overlooked, and they needed a renewed sense of direction. The organization had become very me-oriented. The retail leadership had changed its focus from taking care of people to taking care of itself. Everyone was talking about *me* instead of *we*. No one was looking at the big question: Who are we and what are we here to do?

The me orientation was showing up in the results, the company's integrity, and the emotional health of the organization. Me, me, me. Consequently, the financials were starting to stagnate.

I did the only thing I knew how to do. I went out to all the department heads and said, "We need to become partners. We need to be one team. Forget about divisions. We need to come together as one organization with one purpose to serve our customers and each other. I need you or one of your people to join me on a team that's going to be about *we*, not *me*. The people don't need to report directly to me." I assured the department heads that these team members would come back to tell them what we were up to.

At our first team meeting I explained, perhaps somewhat dramatically and emotionally, that we were going to meet together and work together and live or die together to achieve our goals. Through it all we were going to be inclusive and focused on "the big we" and the big dream of why we're here.

I knew we needed to ground ourselves in the two things that matter at Starbucks no matter what—the coffee and the people. The first thing we did was to start every meeting with a coffee tasting. This kept us focused on our art. The second thing we did was to focus on the human beings we serve, our customers. We did that by having all fifteen of us read a letter that had come in. It was the good, the bad, and of course the ugly. Sometimes it was painful to read those tough letters, sometimes it was wonderful. But it kept us attuned to our primary purpose of being of service to others.

I knew we needed to do more than talk together; we needed to act together. We needed a big common goal that would scare us and challenge us at the same time, one that would bring us together. This is where tactics came into play. I pulled a plan out of thin air. The goal was to grow our average new store volume by $100,000 in three years. At the time, our average volume per new store was almost $650,000. I thought to myself that if we got halfway toward our goal, it would be fantastic.

I had no idea how we'd meet this target. When the team asked me how I came up with the number, I told them: "I made it up, but I believe we can do it." I knew that each person had a role to play, and it wasn't just about numbers. I explained: "Each of you in human resources, you can figure out how to make sure we've got the right people in the right positions, with the right skill sets, and help them to grow. Those of you in the supply chain need to make sure we have the right materials at the right time. Even legal, you have a role to play by acting as a counselor to the group."

A lot of the weight was on the backs of the operations and marketing people. I turned my attention to the merchandising group, which is responsible for all the noncoffee items sold in the stores: "I want you to tell me, of this $100,000, what are you going to contribute in three years?" There was a lot of moaning and complaining. Some people suggested that this approach would put them in competition with each other. More than one manager was angry with me, saying, "Isn't your big idea for us to talk about *we*? Aren't we friends and partners?"

I have never felt that friendly competition in the service of the greater purpose takes away from the individual or greater good. We need to live by our values and produce results. We don't get to choose. At Starbucks, the people who got the best results and helped us to meet our goal would get the most resources. There was no other way to do it, because we were after the *we,* the big goal, not the individual ones.

At a planning session, everybody presented what they were going to do. We challenged each other and, most important, we made commitments to one another. One of the questions that came up was, How do we get the rest of the company to support our plan? In our meetings, we'd been calling the goal "100 in 3." So we ran with that. We put signs around the whole building that just said "100 in 3." People started asking, "What's this 100 in 3?" It got everybody talking and sharing even more ideas. We put signs up throughout the field organization, too. Everybody got on board.

Looking back, two decisions really stand out. Each one tested our sense of what was right and what was true to our larger purpose. First, Jim Alling, head of retail operations, said, "I think we can increase business by adding more people at the times we need them and making sure they're there at the right time."

In essence, he was advocating an increase in labor costs, which went against the prevailing wisdom in retail—to control labor costs. It's the biggest controllable you have in a food-service organization, and most people would say wait until you get the business to get the labor. Here this executive wanted to add the labor because he thought it could increase the business. We went for it.

The other decision was much more controversial—and still is. Semi-automated espresso machines. At the time, our machines weren't automated, although they automated parts of the process. Howard Schultz hated them, because he thought they took away from the romance of our core coffee business. But when we thought about our shared goal of 100 in 3 and looked at our core values—a people business serving coffee—the decision about automation became obvious. Our reasoning went as follows:

1. Quite a few of our people are experiencing carpal tunnel syndrome. We can't continue to do damage to our people.
2. Our customers were saying we were too slow. With increased automation, we can increase service. We can have good service with speed.
3. There was tremendous inconsistency in the quality of our drinks. Increased automation would elevate the quality of our products. We could make a better drink faster.

We were no longer stuck in our underwear struggling with our individual problems and results. We were dealing with our big goals and meeting the real needs of our customers and ourselves.

So what was the end of the story? What did the team produce? It wasn't the 100 in 3 we originally set out to accomplish. It was an amazing 150 in 3. Under the leadership of Jim Donald, who took over the reins from me and saw the initiative through, average store revenue increased by $150,000 in three years. We had set a huge goal, a stretch goal, and Jim and his team blew it away.

Truthfully, I thought if we achieved a $50,000 increase in same-store sales, it would be amazing. Think about it. Same rent, almost the same labor. I knew we could get 50. There was $50,000 lying on the ground. But that 100 in 3 was just a dream. It wasn't grounded in reality. It didn't need to be. It was grounded in hope and driven by a greater purpose—the purpose of people and the greater we.

You Are Bigger Than Your Job Title

Bob Dylan had it right. You gotta serve somebody. You also gotta serve your true self. If you choose a job just for the title that just might be all you get out of it. If you follow your passion and greater purpose, the rewards will be much more meaningful, and you'll make a bigger impact.

It takes a lot of energy for greatness, and it has to be the right fit. But if you put your titles, credit, or even self-protection first, you'll never put your heart into the job. You'll be managing your résumé, not leading yourself. You'll never see the real gold in the opportunity; you'll only be chasing fool's gold. Sometimes you just have to trust yourself and take a chance on a job, project, or opportunity that might not be the most glamorous or résumé-enhancing choice.

The flip side of passing over an opportunity because it doesn't have the right title attached to it is taking a job that just doesn't fit who you are or what you believe in, for the sole purpose of building your résumé. The temptation is always there to adapt to the context around us. This flexibility and ability to learn quickly is a blessing, given the pace of life today. But it is a curse when it makes it too easy for us to drift from our purpose and our one hat. We get bored, we lose motivation, we burn out, or we just lose passion for what we do. We suffer, our jobs suffer, our companies suffer, the people around us really suffer. There is a lesson here for bosses as well as individuals. Hiring people who are résumé-ing their way to the top can undermine your success, too. It leads to a culture of me, not we.

Personal leadership is about tapping into your passion and purpose and making sure they are aligned with your work. Your motivation to lead yourself and others comes from seeing the possibilities to make a difference. When we get stuck thinking about immediate and external rewards, like titles and corner offices, instead of our own deeper priorities, we cut ourselves off from the kinds of things that bring us joy. I've never believed that titles motivate. Seeing possibilities motivates. Results motivate. Making a difference motivates.

The Hundredth-Monkey Effect:
The Power of Doing the Right Thing

The tale of the Hundredth Monkey can inspire us to make a difference in our corner of the world. It reminds us of the power of one person doing something right, which can spread quickly to change the behavior and culture of a whole team. As the story goes, researchers in the 1950s on the island of Koshima, where there was a large population of monkeys, left sweet potatoes in the sand for the monkeys to eat. One clever young monkey discovered she could wash the sand from the tasty vegetables by putting them in the stream. She taught her siblings to do this, and then her playmates, who in turn taught others.

For years, only members of these monkey families washed sand off the sweet potatoes. Then something amazing happened. One day, seemingly overnight, all the monkeys on the island were washing the sweet potatoes. It was as if a certain threshold was reached. Once the hundredth monkey learned the behavior, popularizers of the research explained, it spread to every single monkey on the island. At the time, there were people who believed that the behavior even traveled to monkeys on other islands. It's not like one monkey e-mailed all the others, "wash the potatoes." When a critical mass was reached, they all just knew to do it.

Ken Keyes told this story in the 1980s in the context of the Cold War and the movement to end nuclear proliferation. Although a review of the original research has shown that the change in behavior was more limited, the underlying observation of a cultural shift starting with individual behavior is still valid today. The story of the hundredth monkey reminds us that each of us has an influence on others. It's not always clear who the leaders are and when they'll be able to show their full abilities.

We lead and make a difference by doing what is right. You can make lots of things happen if you don't worry about who gets the credit. Sometimes you're able to go to your boss or one of your leaders, and the person will say, "OK, let's try it." Other times, the first person you speak to doesn't take you up on your idea and you need to persist. Almost everything at Starbucks that's been successful has started with one person doing something that seemed right. This is what happened with the invention of Frappuccino, with the music we play, produce, and sell, and even with the nonfat milk we offer in our drinks, which are stories unto themselves.

Starbucks partners might try something, share their ideas, find other people who embrace them, and eventually contribute to the success their community, in this case Starbucks. Although a specific individual may not get credit for an innovation, the success of *we* comes back like a magnet. The credit may not be for that particular idea, but I believe in the old adage, the more you give, the more you get.

If There Was No Praise in the World

We all need praise and recognition. We all need to feel cared about. It turns out that this trait is actually hardwired into us. Praise and recognition trigger the release of chemicals in our brains, and from them we feel pleasure. Researchers have found that some of us need more praise than others, and we all have insecurities from time to time. It's easy to feel that people just don't know how good you and your contributions are. But you can't wait for someone's approval.

In my thirties, I heard someone ask the question, "If there was no praise or criticism in the world, then who would you be?" This is such a powerful concept. It became one of the first quotes I framed and hung on my wall. I learned that when you discover the answer to that question, you've discovered your greater purpose and the path you need to take.

If you are in a place where your values fit, you're better set than most to take on challenges and succeed. Even if you're doing a difficult task, you'll have a foundation of trust and security that comes from knowing that you are in the right place.

By taking more risks, you can often achieve greater things. If you need a pep talk, reach out and get it. Don't wait for someone to come to you. If no one around you is in a position to act as your mentor, give yourself your own pep talk. Ultimately, you have to do the work—the responsibility lies with you.

> **If there were no praise or criticism in the world, then who would you be? When you can answer that question, you are "there."**

Do You Fit?

At Starbucks we are passionate about hiring partners who think big, who want to have an impact, and who share our values and our mission. We don't want résumé builders or passive dreamers. We want people who will determine what part of the dream is theirs, what part of the dream they can own. What we do is push to the foreground the notion of knowing why we're here. This way, individual and organizational successes are one and the same. We look for people who are passionate about Starbucks and what they can accomplish with us. (If you ever interview for a job at Starbucks, show a bit of your passion and purpose and accept, if offered, a Starbucks drink—hot or cold, caffeinated or not, straight or blended, or even some Tazo tea.)

All companies have cultures where individuals may or may not thrive. Our very ability to lead can be determined by that sense of fit and shared purpose. I agree with the description of visionary companies that was made in *Built to Last:* "Only those who 'fit' extremely well with the core ideology and demanding standards of a visionary company will find it a great place to work. If you go to work at a visionary company, you will either fit and flourish—probably couldn't be happier—or you will likely be expunged like a virus. It's binary. There's no middle ground. It's almost cultlike. Visionary companies are so clear about what they stand for and what they're trying to achieve that they simply don't have room for those unwilling or unable to fit their exacting standards."

When we began our international expansion, we made a commitment to the board and the rest of the people at the company that in five years we'd be profitable, and we wouldn't be a drag on the company. With that understanding, we set out to share our dream with a wider world.

We started with a purpose: to use Starbucks to build bridges among people. And that was it. In one day, I went from having a team of ten thousand people to a team of zero. I was starting over. I had to find people who would join me in making this dream a reality. Three or four positions were all that we were starting with: I needed to recruit a person from finance, one from operations, someone to lead the join-venture selection process, and a person to handle our marketing needs. The company was fully committed to the effort with support and funding, and I saw these jobs as huge opportunities that would grow into something great for the people who would sign on. I was committed to finding as many people as I could from inside the company.

Many people wouldn't make the transfer because the international business unit, if you could call it that, was so small. An awful lot of people weren't willing to take the risk. They wanted security and positions with set job descriptions and titles. And there were people who were more focused on building their résumés than on building the business.

The first person I tried to recruit in the finance role said he would only do it if he got a raise and a VP title, but I felt this was putting the cart before the horse. I tried a second person, someone who seemed to have a sense of purpose in his life, and I knew he was passionate about Starbucks. Fortunately he seized on the challenge and became integral to the success of international, so much so that he was named a vice president at the appropriate time and is now one of the most senior finance people in all of Starbucks.

On the marketing side, early on, I hired a smart, passionate manager from outside the company. She shared the same values as Starbucks and had the skills, experience, perspective, and creativity we needed to help us build our brand around the world. However, while we were innovating daily, what we most needed were processes and guidelines to help manage our rapid multi-country expansion.

When she figured out what was most important to her and why she had come on board, she realized that with such a lean team her dreams and goals for herself were not in sync with where Starbucks was in our development. She realized that she was not the person to build our systems; her passion was to work on big sweeping ideas that would grow our business around the world. Making a very difficult decision, she left the company to pursue her dream somewhere else. For this manager, Starbucks did not end up being the home it is to me, but it was a place to find and test who she was. I still see her, so I know that she went on to thrive in her next endeavors and that she still loves Starbucks. I was proud of her for making the right decision—to honor her one hat.

It's funny, I think of so many people for whom Starbucks is exactly the place to build their dreams. For others who have moved on, sometimes painfully, to something else, we served a different purpose. We pushed people to know why they are here and sometimes, too, why they don't belong here.

Some have found that it just doesn't fit with the way they wanted to live their lives or the hat they chose to wear. Over the years, we've lost a lot of great people because of that, but I think we've kept a lot more. The people who left have gone on to other organizations and have been more productive and happier people because they've actively sought out places that are a better fit. We push people to see what really matters to them—not just professionally, but personally. Starbucks isn't for everybody. No organization is. If you're not able to work on your dreams, if you're only working on work, you're not in the right place.

When You're in a Hole, Quit Digging

It took me a long time to figure out that when I didn't fit, I needed to get out. I had always believed that persistence pays. But I've learned that persistence only pays when your hat fits.

When I left the furniture business, which I knew from top to bottom, to join Thousand Trails, a new type of real estate company, it felt right, smelled right, and sounded right. If people were what I loved, then taking a leadership role in a company that helped people experience great outdoor vacations in beautiful surroundings seemed like the right leap of faith.

In working with our customers, I learned that they were unbelievably passionate about what we were doing. They were not simply Thousand Trails members, they were a community. They shared interests in the outdoors, family time, and friendship. They planned vacations together in different locations, and they felt they were part of our effort as a company to expand the idea to more people and places. I saw that the company was far more valuable than just the product: It was what our product represented in people's lives. We weren't selling memberships; we were offering safety, beauty, and togetherness. I began to think that every work environment could be a community.

Unfortunately, our company was struggling for its economic life, and its current president had recently resigned. I wrote a letter to the chairman and CEO and the members of the board, telling them that I wanted to become the president of the firm. I explained to them all the reasons I thought I was the right person for the job. To my surprise, they said yes.

I had a vision to take the whole business to another level by shifting its corporate focus from a high-pressure sales organization to a sales-and-service one. I started working right away to turn my theory into a reality.

This was a next-to-impossible feat, however, as time was short and the board and investors were positioning the company for a sale. Even worse, I was lousy at moving from the head of operations to the sales environment of my new role. It demanded that I put the sales line ahead of my values. The more I tried to do the job, the less successful I was at it.

For two stressful and frustrating years, I struggled with a job I just couldn't get done. Yet I wouldn't give up. I kept digging. My results were suffering, and so was I. The truth is that I grew my protest beard, which I still have, in hopes that I would get fired. It was not very mature, but it certainly worked. It was a defining moment in my life.

If you need to leave a job, it doesn't mean you are a quitter. If something is in conflict with your values, you should own up to it and revisit your one hat. Personal leadership starts and ends with knowing yourself and knowing where you're going, and why. Own up to what's not right, and do something about it.

Once I left the real-estate company, it felt as if a fog around me slowly lifted. I started to reflect in a deeper way on my accomplishments, failures, and dreams. There was a current of understanding I began to see. It was not always the product that was sold that could make the world a better place. Most of the time it was the people and the way the company was run.

I was beginning to see that you can change your corner of the world, not just by inventing something that doesn't pollute or cures a disease but also by running a company that is a good and decent place to work. I was having glimpses of this idea—service, community, and the sense of something bigger than ourselves—and soon enough I'd have another chance to put that belief into action.

Leading with One Hat at Starbucks

At Starbucks, I've known since day one why I was here. When Howard Schultz met with me to talk about working at Starbucks, he was looking for a person to head up operations at his fledgling coffee company. The job description called for someone with a traditional business education—hopefully someone with an MBA from a top school, with multiunit food-service experience, who would help him grow the company.

Although Starbucks was small in size, it was big in ambition, investor expectations, and certainly in potential. There were just twenty-eight stores in the northwestern United States and Canada, and a few locations in Chicago, and the company was not yet profitable. Howard Schultz was looking to create a senior management team to give the young company the leadership capacity it needed to go forward. I had plenty of experience, but it was all on the job. No MBA. No white shirt. Not even a college degree. My education was watching, listening, imitating, and doing.

Perhaps it was the coincidence of age or the collection of other experiences or the other people who converged at Starbucks at the same time that led us to come together. I was looking for a place to work where I could eliminate the borders between my personal and professional selves and where success and dreams would be one and the same. That's when I think I may just be really lucky, or perhaps I did something right in a previous life.

Starbucks took a chance on me, and I took a chance on Starbucks. We both took the leap, not because of my résumé or their prestige but because we saw we had come from different directions to a common dream—one that had not yet been articulated—which was to nurture and inspire the human spirit.

For me, pushing or prodding or helping others see their potential is my single desire in life, and it is the force that gives my life purpose. The Starbucks team put the words to it, and I've made them my own.

I don't know of a single other company that has grown in such a human way, with all of the mistakes and imperfections and hurt feelings and misunderstandings experienced right along with the glorious celebrations. We accomplished something we could have never imagined, and we did it because we were all there for the same reason.

So, without the degrees, the white shirt, or the multiunit food-service experience, I got an opportunity that most others never get.

Surprise, surprise. I didn't need that MBA. For many people, that's the best route, but in the end, whether degreed or not, it's our knowing who we are and why we're here that makes all the difference.

EXTRA SHOTS: Know Why You're Here

- Why are you in this job? This organization? This life?

- Are you looking in the right place to dig? Where can you put your passion, your spade, in the ground? It's your life.

- Are you spending more time on tactics and the little stuff and not enough time on the big stuff—on goals, strategy, and people?

- Is there a place in your work where you're "lost in your underwear"? How can you get to a higher level?

- Are you considering a new opportunity at your current job or somewhere new? Does it fit your passion, not just your résumé? Does it fit your values?

- Do you know what matters and motivates your people as individuals, as a team? Find out. Find out more.

- Ask yourself, If there was no praise or criticism in the world, then who would I be?

3. THINK INDEPENDENTLY

The Person Who Sweeps the Floor Should Choose the Broom

Most of us have jobs that are too small for our spirit.

—STUDS TERKEL, QUOTING AN INTERVIEWEE
IN *WORKING*

Everybody *wants* to experience fulfillment in the work they do and in their lives. Without the engagement and creativity of their people, organizations cannot succeed. Successful organizations *require* these qualities. Yet it is in the very nature of organizations to stifle their people, to order them around, to tell them what to do. It's all too easy to get caught up in following the rule book rather than meeting the true needs of the people we serve.

Recipes Not Rules

At Starbucks Coffee we work hard to create a culture of independence where partners at every level can make their own on-the-job decisions. Our mission is to empower each person to bring his or her unique perspective and skills to the job. We want people to take charge instead of blindly following a rigid set of instructions from a rule book. However, when a company is growing fast, there is a tendency to come up with rules to try to get people up to speed quickly. Similarly, more rules can seem like a solution when an organization is trying to contain costs, deal with slowed growth, or address problems that are not clearly defined or understood. Rules, systems, and procedures are natural tactics, and often they can help ensure good things.

Unfortunately, in many cases, the rule book goes way too far—it tries to tell people how to be instead of explaining what we're trying to do. Rule books don't empower, they disempower people. We need recipes, not rules. Unsurprisingly, the me culture that led to stagnating same-store sales during a period of change and expansion at Starbucks also set in motion a rules culture designed to manage the stress of change and undefined challenges.

People thought they were doing all the right stuff. And on the surface it certainly seemed like they were. There were logical-sounding systems and organizational layers in place. One day when I was out in the field, I walked into the back room of a Starbucks store and saw a sign that said BE NICE. BE FAST. BE CLEAN. I looked at that sign and said sarcastically, "Well, that's really motivational! What about a sign that says, BE HUMAN?

Ideally, management should never tell someone *how* to do something or *what to feel*. If people's every last action is dictated to them, they are robbed of their dignity, and the company is robbed of its soul.

There Is No Rule Book for Being Human

In order to run a successful business, particularly a large international company, guidelines are necessary. You need to set quality standards for products. A good example of this is a recipe for a drink. A double tall vanilla latte has to taste the same in Tokyo as it does in Baton Rouge. It's also important that some things are done in certain ways in order to maintain safety. Stores might have a specific protocol that needs to be followed during closing to help protect the partners against possible theft or injury. These instructions can be viewed as tools that people can use for the good of the customers and themselves, instead of rules that rob them of their ability to think and act independently.

I prefer to think of the guidelines we need as a set of standards or expectations. Explain to people what you expect of them, and they will surprise you and go beyond what you could ever have imagined.

Rules drive me crazy. When things are rule bound, people stop pleasantly surprising you, and more, they stop trusting themselves. The truth is, it's not possible to train every person by breaking down every possible task or situation into totally prescribed steps. It's a worthless investment. Instead of writing manuals that lock people into dehumanizing behavior, we should focus on outcomes we want and the reasons behind them. At Starbucks, it doesn't take a rule book to know that our goal is to enthusiastically satisfy the people we serve.

This approach doesn't just apply to everyday tasks. It is an enormously valuable concept that can be applied to the way people work together in every kind of organization. In my experience, when you gain agreement on what needs to be accomplished, the people on your team will always find a good way to do it. This is especially true when we talk about human issues—all the things people do with other people, like serving, negotiating, planning, and dealing with colleagues. Creating tool books instead of rule books grows people's spirits. It allows us to be productively human. As Studs Terkel, the social historian and workers' philosopher, said in quoting one of his interviewees, "Most of us have jobs that are too small for our spirit." Leaders have an obligation to grow people's spirits for the good of the organization and for the good of the individual. In other simple yet equally powerful terms, the poet Marge Piercy wrote, "The pitcher cries for water to carry and a person for work that is real."

People Are Not Assets

Contrary to common business-speak, people are not assets. You own assets. You don't own people. Assets are buildings and trucks and supplies. Assets are things. Every so many seconds or minutes, a machine spits a product out. Or you flip a switch, and the lights go on. Assets always give us what we expect—unless a piece of equipment breaks down. People never quite give us what we expect. People surprise us because it's in the very nature of being human. We even surprise ourselves.

I don't do the same thing every day. I get off track. I think of something new or change my mind. Often for the better, but not always. As human beings, we're always changing and always moving, depending on where we are at that particular moment in time. It's helpful for us to recognize this in ourselves and in the people around us.

I like to think of a business as a group of volunteers who lease their creativity for the good of the organization. When any of us, from staff to managers to the CEO, think of ourselves and our colleagues as people—not workers or assets—we discover a wealth of knowledge and talent. When we allow ourselves and others to think creatively and make independent decisions based on common goals, we become more fulfilled, and we make a more worthwhile contribution.

Honor Independent Thinking

At Starbucks, we want local leadership to practice leadership courage. Though it's a challenge for store managers or field leadership to always hit the mark when they are reacting so quickly to all the demands on the ground and, of course, from the Seattle support center, most of the time they get it right and the results are often powerful and long lasting.

During our launch into the Toronto market, our real estate team had the good fortune to lease a site with a coveted boulevard patio license in a small neighborhood in the center of the city. The landlord had told us that the lease for the current tenant was up (which it was) and that the tenant did not want to renew. Once the agreement with Starbucks had been negotiated, the landlord informed the tenant. Surprise, surprise, we found out the tenant did not want to move and he started to tell his customers. Although we had the best of intentions, the unfortunate situation created a negative image of Starbucks and the story was picked up by the local media.

Because the landlord had assured us that the current tenant wanted out of the lease, our Seattle team thought the whole thing would blow over. But the instincts of the local leader at the time, Roly Morris, told him otherwise. He made a decision to move proactively to address the situation.

Roly drafted a heartfelt, personal letter, which he inserted as a full-page advertisement in the city's largest newspaper. It cost $25,000, but he and his team felt it was the best way to reach the people they wanted to serve. The letter reminded people that Starbucks, too, had started as a small business years earlier in the Pike Place market and that we had a desire to be a productive part of the community. The open letter made clear that we'd be happy to give our lease to the existing café owner.

A few months later, with the situation resolved, the Toronto team decided to place a second open letter in the same newspaper, for an additional $25,000. This second letter explained exactly what we promised to do and how things had turned out, including the arrangement for the current café to stay in the space.

At the end of the day, because of the decision of the local management team, our reputation stayed intact. Their actions set a standard for worrying less about the rule book and more about doing the right thing, even if there were risks involved. It showed not only the people of Toronto but everyone in the Starbucks community what our values were and the lengths we would go to live up to them.

The Person Who Sweeps the Floor
Should Choose the Broom

It's not only executives and managers who should feel empowered to make their own decisions, but all people throughout an organization. After all, who is better equipped to choose the broom than the guy who sweeps the floor?

Many companies are so bogged down with management and organizational layers that decisions directly affecting the day-to-day of an individual's job are often made without his or her input. Ideally, everyone who will be affected by a particular decision or change should be involved in the process at some level or should have their views taken into consideration. Once everyone has come to an agreement about what needs to be accomplished, then the people with the hands-on expertise can follow through in the most effective way.

In the case of brooms, the people who know about things like getting the best price for brooms and how many the whole company will need can enter the picture and perhaps select five brooms that make sense from a purchasing perspective. But why in the world would you want to leave the final selection to the person sitting back in the purchasing department, when he or she will never touch it? The person who uses the broom should decide which one to buy.

In your own sphere of influence and relationships, you can practice independent thinking and encourage others to think independently. Rather than experiencing a loss of control, you'll experience an immediate gain in the commitment of the people around you and increased satisfaction and productivity in the work you do together.

Independence Comes with Knowing Why You're Here

Once, during a store visit, I saw a customer approach a barista and explain that he didn't like the drink he had just purchased. The customer wanted a new drink. To make the customer feel satisfied, the barista opened the till and handed the customer a cash refund and then commenced to make the customer a new drink. Was that the best response? From a purely economic point of view, obviously not.

The way we teach people to handle a situation like this is to apologize and offer to remake the drink. There's a good chance the customer would have been satisfied and everyone would have benefited. He didn't have to give the money back. But this response was better than a lot of others. It was an honest, care-filled exchange, and the barista demonstrated that he understood and appreciated the most important element of his role: human service. In the business of life, what can be wrong with that?

It's really as simple as this. As long as you know why you're here, as long as all of you together know why the organization exists, you'll get where you need to go.

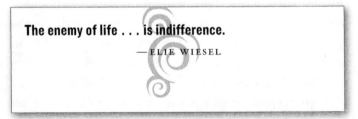

The enemy of life . . . is indifference.

— ELIE WIESEL

Develop Trust in Yourself

Each of us has an obligation to ourselves and our organizations to think independently. Personal leadership demands it of us. Independent thinking is a human quality that is part of us, not something that can be given to you or taken away on the whim of a boss or rule maker. I'm not talking about anarchism or me-ism. But say you're a young product manager who comes to a company shortly after graduation from college. You see and learn things, and you get an idea for something your department ought to try out, but roadblocks hamper your efforts. Perhaps your boss is preoccupied with a number of other pressing issues and doesn't want to take time to think the idea through.

I believe, even if you're new to the organization, you need to be assertive when it comes to things you believe in. You have to do it with humility, but you've got to be firm. You don't have to go into someone's office and make it a formal occasion. You get lots of opportunities to share your ideas. You can work around the roots of your organization, talking to people with different levels of responsibility than you have. See what they think about the idea and what they suggest. Talk to people in different departments. Go out to lunch with colleagues.

Ideas have a way of bubbling up. Most people think that in order to get something done they have to go to their boss or have to be officially asked. But of course this isn't true. Put the focus on getting something done rather than on who gets the credit, and you will be amazed at the results.

When I became president of Starbucks North America, it was a much bigger operation than when I had left it to start our international company. We had gone from four hundred or so stores to more than two thousand. With a fivefold growth in stores, people, and products, the company became a lot more complex to manage. I kept thinking I had to adjust and live by the rules of a big organization. I'd tell myself, this is how it has to be.

One day Howard Schultz came into my office, and I told him straight out, "I'm not getting this. I'm not being successful. I don't know how to do this." I even threw my glasses across the room in frustration. (Sometimes I was the one calming him down, but that day he was calming me down.)

That night I went home to my wife, Lynn, and said, "You know, I'm not being effective because I'm trying to be something other than me. I've been thinking that because the company is different, I have to be different." I wasn't trusting myself, my values, my hat. Lynn and I sat down and talked, and she reminded me that I can only be who I am. I knew I could learn new skills, but I had to stay true to my values. In essence, I had to set myself free to do what I knew how to do.

I was struggling with one part of the organization that was a "filter"—a multidepartment group that set priorities and approved new initiatives. Of course filters in organizations, whether formal or informal, are needed because they help set priorities, ensuring that we have the right resources at the right times and that we don't overload the baristas and store managers with new products and promotions. It helps focus time and attention when faced with an endless storm of new creative ideas. On the other hand, it can end up stopping a lot of good things, and it can keep you from changing and growing.

Filters can provide structure, but they can also limit growth and stifle necessary change. Filters are inherently conservative, creating tests and barriers for new possibilities. Parents are a bit like filters, but experienced parents learn to change and adapt as part of the natural process of raising children. A parent learns that what a child needs at three isn't the same as what he or she needs at seventeen. To parent well, you had better learn the difference.

At Starbucks, I needed to understand that we were growing and changing, but not, I hoped, at the expense of thinking independently. If I wore my one hat and kept true to my values, I could adapt to what had changed without giving up to the rules and filters that were holding us back. I could lead and guide the company toward the future with independence and integrity.

Canadian Independence

Sometimes as an individual you feel you've lost your way, and you start going through the motions and following the written and unwritten rules. In the short term it can seem right to go along and do things the way everyone else is doing them. The problem is, when a whole group of individuals, a unit, or division starts "going along," there can be a huge negative effect on the organization that multiplies over time. That became the case in Canada.

The Canadian stores were set up as a part of Starbucks North America Retail. In essence, they reported to their geographic counterpart in the United States. That worked well and was certainly efficient when the total number of stores was still small and concentrated in the Pacific Northwest, near the company's Seattle roots.

However, in setting up more systems and hierarchy to manage our growth throughout North America, the needs of the Canadian stores were being overlooked. The Seattle office was ignoring our people there and their sense of their own culture, as well as the very real business and economic differences between the two countries. By seeing them through our own American view of the world, we were actually holding them back.

We made a simple decision to "break the rules," which led to a burst of passion and energy. I decided to hire a president of Canada, Colin Moore. The whole country came together under his leadership. Now they had the ability to set their own goals and create their own dreams. They decided where to open, where to expand, and which piece of the Starbucks dream they could own. It has turned out to be a great example of what independent thinking can accomplish. Canada more than doubled their revenues and doubled the number of stores from 332 to 686 between 2002 and 2006. The results in morale and commitment were nearly immediate, and the momentum has continued to this day.

Trust Yourself—and Entrust Others— to Do What Needs to Be Done

Most people want to do the right thing. When we're trusted to think and act as human beings, our spirits engage, and we're likely to exceed everyone's expectations, including our own. The success of the Nordstrom department store chain can be chalked up to excellent service that is consistent with this philosophy.

My friend Bruce Nordstrom, retired co-chairman of Nordstrom, has it right. He talks about "providing freedom" as the primary job of the employer: freedom to serve, freedom to make decisions right on the spot, and a management willing to live with those decisions. He believes in empowered people who have an entrepreneurial spirit. Regardless of the economic conditions at any particular time, the shopping experience at Nordstrom is like dealing with the familiar owner of a local boutique. That sense of pride and ownership gives people the freedom to serve themselves and the organization.

All of us can try to put this spirit of independence into our own work. I always recommend to people that they try to focus less on what they *should* do, and more on *why* they should do it. If you're doing the right thing, you're not following the rules, you're following your one hat. You know you're doing the right thing when:

- What you want to do, want you're inspired to do, and what the organization, your boss, and your customers want and need you to do are all aligned.
- You can think independently, because you're clear about the larger goal.
- You get the information and authority you need to make better on-the-job decisions. You're able to take control of your life.
- You start asking—and encourage those around you to ask—how your own unique skill set could best serve the task, project, or problem at hand.

There's no better feeling than being encouraged to fully use your abilities. You will find your work far more satisfying, and you'll encourage that same satisfaction in others. Everybody wins.

The more we know ourselves and our goals, the fewer rules are needed. If you're a control freak—and face it, most of us in business are, at some level—this can be scary. We can start to look for rules even when there aren't any. We can look to follow others and find answers from others, and not ourselves. Don't give someone a list of tasks and wonder why "he just doesn't show any passion for his work." Take the time to explain what needs to be done and the reasons why. And trust that that person will begin to take appropriate actions. It is not a risk to put faith in others. It is a risk not to.

The Talk

When new senior leaders come into the Starbucks organization, I try to spend time with them and let them know I'm there to help. I'm only halfway kidding when I say, "I try to get to them first." We have coffee. We talk about the bigger picture of why they joined us and what their role really is.

These talks are not about rules and financial objectives but hopes and dreams and the freedom to live the values of Starbucks and make a contribution. We talk about why they were hired and what they are here to do: to serve their one hat, to serve the goals of Starbucks, and to find the piece of Starbucks they can own. Most of all, I use these conversations to share one of the most basic but powerful beliefs at Starbucks: The guy who sweeps the floor should choose the broom. I ask them to think wisely but act independently. Or put another way—know why you're here, and act accordingly.

EXTRA SHOTS: Think Independently

- Is your work and life filled with recipes or rules? Which rules do you need? Which can you throw away?

- Are rules—real and perceived—keeping you from changing and growing—personally? In your organization?

- Can you speak your mind freely? Even if your opinion goes against rules? Are you receptive to free thinking from those around you?

- As a leader, how can you encourage people to question the stated and unstated rules in the organization?

- How are you encouraging the people around you to use all of their abilities? Are you treating people as assets or humans?

4. BUILD TRUST

Care, Like You Really Mean It

> People don't care how much you know. They want
> to know how much you care.
>
> — FAMILIAR SAYING

don't know if there are any MBA programs that have courses
entitled "How to Love 101" or "The Caring Workplace," but
there should be. It's impossible to lead in business—or in
life—unless you genuinely care about people. That's what
matters. Period.

My experience working at every level of business—from
being the guy who set up and cleaned furniture showrooms to
being president of a multibillion-dollar international company—
is that it's much more important to lead with your heart than
with your head. Love and trust are the universal motivators. And
there's no trust without caring.

When I talk about caring, I'm talking about putting other people before yourself—not just the bosses and colleagues and staff you work with every day, but all the people inside your organization, as well the people in the outside world whom you serve, including customers and suppliers. Caring about people keeps you focused on what truly matters.

Show, Don't Just Tell

A casual "love ya" tossed at a spouse upon leaving the house in the morning, without a warm hug and a look into each other's eyes, can be an empty gesture. So, too, is caring in the workplace, unless we have the actions and results that go with it. We have to "Care, like we mean it." It's something that we need to practice every day.

You show caring when:

- You start with yourself and appreciate and take pleasure in your positive results and daily experiences; you are authentically vulnerable. You invite feedback when you know in your heart of hearts that your performance is not what it should be.
- You appreciate others, say thank you, and acknowledge contributions wherever they come from. When an individual's performance isn't meeting expectations, you offer honest, truthful, and timely feedback and deliver it in a positive and caring way. You do not wait for review time to give authentic feedback.
- You take responsibility for giving and receiving honest appreciation and coaching. You understand that caring, as an

aspect of leadership, isn't solely a hierarchical event. Just as experience travels in both directions, so does caring. The expert and the novice both have something to contribute. The advice and support of your friend or your spouse can be just as important and meaningful as the insight and direction of the VP who has been in the organization for ten years.

You can be sure not caring is just as powerful as caring. Without caring you can't become an outstanding performer. You may not always get back the caring you give—it's not a quid pro quo. But you can't possibly build an organization that cares if you don't care. The whole world knows the difference. At the level of the individual, your colleagues, peers, and customers can feel your lack of commitment. At the level of the global corporation, when you don't care, the reputation you aspire to is undermined by gossip and stories that are the exact opposite of the ones you want to be known for.

Once, at a Starbucks leadership meeting, somebody asked the question, "We have over a hundred thousand people at Starbucks now. How can we possibly expect all of us to care?" And my answer back was, "How can we not?"

When Did Caring Become a Dirty Word?

For some unimaginable reason, most corporations are biased against showing care in the workplace. It always strikes me as one of the most ironic things in business when I see recruiting brochures or letters from the CEO stress "care" as a core company value, but then the company acts in a way that is 180 degrees from the words they espoused.

We seem to admire the stoic, the person with a great poker face, the stone-faced negotiator. Caring is one of our most powerful resources, but often we don't reward and elevate the leaders who master the ability to use it appropriately. The difference between an average manager and a great manager is that the latter understands that we can't hide our caring and still be genuine or effective. If we don't truly care about other people and have the guts to show it—even when things go badly—our humanity disappears. We have to remember that it's always about the people. We may be rewarded for the results we achieve in the organization, but we'll never know the results we *might* have achieved if we truly showed we cared. Results without caring are empty results. They're just not sustainable.

You Can't Fake It

Caring isn't easy, and it isn't the same as being nice. We hired a young manager to work on strategy at Starbucks. He was one of the smartest people you'll ever meet. He was sharp, and his analysis would always wow you. He'd figure out what needed to get done, and then he'd press forward to get the necessary results. So what was the problem? He was always out of kilter with the people on his team, and they complained that he was difficult to work with.

Sometimes, however, personal leadership requires that we care more about others than we perceive others to care for us. If the results are there, if the commitment is there, if no one is being harmed, as leaders and team members we need to give our care without waiting for it to be returned.

With this manager's knowledge, I went around to all his people and asked if they thought he cared about the business and cared about them—even if he didn't show it, or didn't show it in the way they wanted him to. To a person, no one doubted his abilities or the fact that they mattered. I asked each team member to speak up to the manager when they felt ignored or hurt. I asked them to take responsibility for caring—and they came through. Over time, he took on several big projects and achieved outstanding financial results for the company. Was he a perfect human being? No. But in the end, the people were able to move past their expectations of how they wanted things to be. They were able to set aside their focus on *me* to create a larger *we*.

It needs to be repeated: People are not assets. Caring isn't just about admiring the charismatic leaders, the people that everybody likes, or the in crowd. This is the big caring we do that shows we "care, like we really mean it." It's about words and actions that everybody sees and recognizes. There's an old adage that says, "People don't care how much you know, they want to know how much you care."

Letters from the Front Lines

In the early years of Starbucks, we were really focused on being coffee experts. In fact, some people perceived us as arrogant and maybe even coffee snobs. We knew that we made great coffee and that a great product was one of the keys to building a great company. So it was a wake-up call when I came back from a trip one time to find three letters complaining about Starbucks customer service.

These letters weren't about the coffee . . . they were about the people. They were complaining about the human side of the equation. Lapses in service can happen in any organization, no matter what its size, but these letters went deeper than complaints about a particular store or person. Each of these letters was written with a lot of care and feeling, and each one went to the heart of our values, our one hat. One letter was particularly vivid, saying, "I love your coffee and I go into your store every day. But I want to be treated like a human being who matters. Apparently customers are not important to you."

It was the beginning of recognizing that we're not just a coffee company, we're a human service company. We were learning that "good service is hands and feet, but great service is heart." I decided to write a note to all the store managers throughout the organization, explaining to them how these letters made me feel. I wanted them to know that I was sad and disappointed that we hadn't showed we cared. I asked for their thoughts and ideas on what we could do to build a truly caring organization.

We decided to invite the managers of the specific stores involved *and* our customers, the three people who wrote the letters, to come together to talk. We didn't have a particular agenda or message in mind, but we knew that if we were able to get people together, the power of human connection would triumph. Sometimes I think, despite all the imperfection and the mistakes we've made, that's really the essence of Starbucks. If we have a problem, we bet on the human spirit and believe that when people come together, face-to-face, the human connection wins out.

When the customers talked, the results were emotional and powerful. It was crystal clear that we had become too wrapped up in the coffee and our knowledge of it, to the exclusion of the real business we were in—the business of people. Our love for coffee was clear to us, but our love for people was not clear to ourselves or our customers. We got swept up in our passion for the product instead of our passion for the people. This was a critical moment in the history of Starbucks. We learned that caring mattered and that we could never take it for granted. It reminded us what we were really about.

> **Many people will walk in and out of your life, but only true friends will leave footprints in your heart.**
>
> — ELEANOR ROOSEVELT

Caring Every Day: The Half-Life of Relationships

Showing you care is a way to make sure that you keep people with you on your journey through life. Caring creates trust. If you don't want to take my word for it, for just one week, every time your spouse or significant other says, "I love you," mumble some unintelligible response. I guarantee you'll have a conversation by the end of that week. You could be married for twenty-five years and have raised four children and two dogs, and you will still have a conversation at the end of the week. Relationships break down incredibly fast because of one simple thing: Other people don't trust that you care. Now, can you imagine how fast trust breaks down in a business, without the glue of committed relationships and community to hold it together?

None of us should go a day, a week, or a month without some form of genuine communication with the people we care about. Don't wait until there's a problem. When you wait, people think you don't care. Open, honest attention and dialogue is the glue of healthy relationships. Without caring, relationships don't last—at work or at home.

Do the Right Thing

As Rabbi Hillel's saying goes: "If not me, who? And if not now, when?"

It doesn't matter who you are, if you care, you pick up the cigarette butts. You pick up the straws and the straw wrappers. If you see a Starbucks cup, you stop your car and pick it up. And you pick up the other stuff there, too. (OK, it is truth time . . . sometimes I have left the McDonald's ones.) That piece of paper with the Starbucks name on it reflects on all of us at Starbucks. When you pick it up, you set an example. Even when no one is looking. Even when it's not comfortable.

It's the same with people.

Let's say there's a mistake, there are unexpected losses, and the company chairman or president or division head comes roaring in, saying, "How could you have let that happen? How can you keep the person who did that here?" The leader needs to stand between the bullet and the person it's aimed at. You might feel it's easier to say, "Fine, I'll go fix that problem. I'll let that person go." But the positive results that come from the boss standing in front of a bullet are immeasurable. That kind of caring drives an organization. People will go anywhere and do anything for the person who cares like they really mean it—and puts that caring into action.

Never Close the Door

When you start to close the door on anybody, the doors close on everybody. I'm not talking about your office door. When you begin to shun or reject one person, your care is compromised. The message gets out as if the slamming sound was on a voice mail broadcast from your office. We need to work at relationships and caring with *all* people.

It's funny, isn't it, how often the people you are closest to are the people you go through the most challenging times with. The desire to overcome adversity is one of the most compelling human drives. Doing so with another person creates an intimate bond. When you face challenges with those you work with, a deep love is created. I have found that I can get through almost anything if I believe the other person cares . . . about me, about themselves, and about our mission.

Yes, leaders set caring in motion. When the doors close, when there's fear, then our attention is on ourselves and not other people. But each of us has to practice the habits of caring the best we can. When you care about others—your favorite people *and* the people that are harder for you to deal with—you can get through the stress and worry. You can handle the mistakes. Your peers and colleagues and customers stick with you to get outstanding results and build outstanding organizations. Caring, big caring, caring like you mean it, isn't in the rule book.

Caring at the Top: H2O

From the beginning, Howard Schultz knew that he wanted to build a different kind of company and that trust—with all the people—would be an essential ingredient. That trust began with the leadership team he brought together to drive and manage our growth and our transition to a national, and, eventually, global organization.

I was brought on board to oversee the stores, the people, and the people systems at Starbucks. Orin Smith was brought on as CFO to establish fiscal systems and manage our financial resources. Always the visionary, Howard drove our market-growth strategy and our ascent to the top of each mountain on the horizon.

It was in these intense years, shortly before going public and through the initial phase of our expansion, that the mood and culture of the company was established. We each had our distinct roles, individual strengths and weaknesses, and of course our own egos. But together we were a perfect fit.

Early on, we got into the habit of meeting on Monday nights to have dinner, compare notes, catch up on our personal lives, and celebrate or commiserate together, depending on what was going on. I remember laughing, crying, talking quietly, and arguing loudly. Every week was different, but through it all what developed was a deep sense of trust and shared values. No matter what the issues were, we grew to care deeply about each other.

That mutual trust and caring transferred and flowed through the rest of the organization. Over time, people in the company coined the term H2O (Howard Howard and Orin) to refer to us. I'm not so sure it's coincidental that the term also means water. There was a flow of communication that made the three of us, and the company, stronger than we would be by ourselves. There was an energy that kept us moving and never allowed us to get stuck.

One of us was always in the right frame of mind to deal with the matter at hand, whether we needed more risk-taking, more caution, or more stability, whether we needed more thought-fulness about our financial picture, more persistence in a new venture, or to put more passion and attention in supporting the people in our stores and the people we served. Like a great bas-ketball team, we could pass the ball without even knowing where we were aiming, and we could count on someone being there to receive the pass.

This trust at the top also meant there was always someone people could talk to. Deidra Wager, who was head of retail op-erations, once told me that whenever there was a major conflict or a crisis between us in the organization, she knew "the H2O alchemy would work" and the situation would be dealt with. She knew we didn't play one off the other, nor did we create our own fiefdoms or organizational structures. A conversation with one of us was a conversation with all of us.

Our leadership goals were never about ourselves as individu-als; they were always about all of us. That clarity has made all the difference. We didn't join Starbucks to build our résumés or our careers. The overarching value the three of us shared was that our people and our customers were more important than we were. That's how we lived. We cared for one another and we extended our care to the whole Starbucks team. We gave them our respect and the security that comes from knowing there is honesty and care at the highest level of the company.

Getting Big and Staying Small

When people know how much you care, they come back. We built Starbucks with a relentless commitment to learning and sharing all we could about our coffee. But we never could have created the

In the high art of serving others, workers sustain their morale, management keeps its customers, and the nation prospers. One of the indisputable lessons of life is that we cannot get or keep anything for ourselves alone unless we also get it for others.

— RICHARD J. SNEED

Starbucks we have without an equally passionate approach to ensuring that our humanity doesn't get lost along the way.

At a certain point in the mid-nineties, when we had grown to the point where we had several thousand employees—up from the hundreds we had had just a few years before—we realized that it was important to figure out how to keep all of us focused on our mission of serving people—all the people. We asked ourselves, how can we keep that sense of personal caring alive, when we can't know everyone in the company?

Around that time we were reminded of the powerful ideas of the economist E. F. Schumacher. In his book *Small Is Beautiful: Economics as if People Mattered*, written in 1973, he wrote: "The fundamental task is to achieve smallness within a large organization." From that, Howard Schultz developed the mantra "staying small while growing big."

When the North American operation was still small, I really wanted to make a big deal of each person. I thought the way to do this was to recognize people for their everyday achievements and to catch people doing the little things right. If someone wanted to recognize a colleague, we'd go to their cubicle or office and say thank you for doing X, Y, or Z, and we'd give them a big showy helium balloon that would bob overhead so everyone on the floor would see it. Any person who observed someone doing something right could celebrate them with a balloon.

It was a fun, joyful, and collectively satisfying way to show one another we cared. We tried to take the idea to the stores, but it was too unwieldy and cumbersome, so we eventually switched to pins to recognize good deeds. Another custom we put in place, which I stole from an early mentor, proved equally worthwhile and has become part of the Starbucks culture worldwide. I sent birthday and company anniversary cards to most everybody in the organization. It started with about sixty cards every month.

By the time I retired, I was sending out more than twenty-five hundred a month. Imagine. Every time I was on an airplane or in front of the television, there I was, signing cards and writing notes. Boxes and boxes of them. Despite the fact that, by the end, it was an overwhelming task, it had become a part of the Starbucks lore and practice of "getting big and staying small." In fact, when I left day-to-day responsibilities at the company, sending cards had taken on a life of its own. Almost all leaders throughout the organization were sending out cards. Today, when I see people around the company, they still come up to me and tell me how much those cards meant to them. The essence of this idea is that we must always find tangible ways to show we care about one another. Though the gesture of sending cards was small, the impact was deep and sustaining.

To deliver the often-complicated orders at Starbucks, the store partners have to really and truly listen. They have to care. This is not a corporate skill. It's a human skill. It's not about coffee, but about connecting with other people. One person and one cup of coffee at a time. I have tried hard to live and lead by the spirit contained in this Chinese proverb: "If you want to build for one year from now, grow wheat. If you want to build for ten years from now, grow trees. If you want to build for one hundred years from now, grow people."

EXTRA SHOTS: Build Trust

- Does your workplace, team, family have a culture of caring? What could you do to make it more so?

- How do *you* show you really care like you mean it at home?

- Do you equate caring with lack of toughness? If so, can you suspend this belief—even for a day or a week?

- What have you done that you're proud of—today—this week—this year?

- What has a coworker or employee done that has helped the whole team get closer to achieving a goal? Did you acknowledge and appreciate this act?

- Is there a place in your organization where you can "act small"? Try it out.

- What part are you playing to build a culture of trust in your organization?

5. LISTEN FOR THE TRUTH

The Walls Talk

> Compassionate emptiness.
> —A BUDDHIST TEACHING

Have you ever been to an art museum and stood before a great work of art? It captivates you and transports you to a new place. The mythologist Joseph Campbell used to call this epiphany an *aesthetic arrest*. The art "stops" you and communicates with you if you let it. The same phenomenon can happen in conversation with another person. When we stop and wait for the meaning and emotions to unfold, we will hear a message. This is communication with heart.

Something similar happens when we're struck by the ambiance when we walk into a particular office, cubicle, home, or store. We sometimes have an immediate sense of peace, unease, or excitement. For many years I've thought of this as "the walls talking."

The Walls of Starbucks Talk

It was my antennae that told me Starbucks would be the right place for me to work. I still remember the day I interviewed with Howard Schultz. We met on a Saturday morning. The offices were in the very first roasting plant, a little old building that smelled of coffee before you entered it. As we walked up the narrow stairs, with Howard walking ahead and not uttering a word, I could feel the energy. When we reached the landing, I could see a few empty cubicles and a Starbucks sign on the wall, but in spite of the silence I was hearing the walls talk.

And so, on that I day, I pretty much knew it was a place I wanted to be. It wasn't what Howard said, though we certainly had a great conversation, it was the feeling that I got. The place had soul.

Antennae Up

When we pay attention, we actually prime our reticular activating system. If you're thinking of buying a new car, say a blue Volvo, everywhere you look you'll see blue Volvos. You'll think it's the most popular model around, even though you never noticed them before. If you've ever done the workshop exercise where you're asked to look for the color yellow in the meeting room, you know that you'll start to see the color everywhere, even though at first glance the room looks like a sea of blue, white, gray, and black.

When you go to work at a new company, some things hit you right away, and other things are hidden until you start to look beneath the surface. Still, when we're new, we're forced to ask a lot more questions, because nothing is automatic. We get lost in the halls. We don't know the whole hierarchy of who's "important" and who's not. We don't know which project is in or out. Our antennae are up. The trick is to keep your antennae up all the time.

That's how my father ran his store, Al Behar Grocery. He always used his antennae to pick up what wasn't being said. He used to tell me stories about the store from the Depression years, and they taught me about the importance of paying attention to all the things the customers weren't saying or asking for. He knew all the people who came into his store, and he could tell how tight money was by the items they selected. Sometimes he'd put a bunch of bananas in a customer's bag, a small gesture to help out those who needed it.

This is an old-fashioned lesson that's just as needed today. You can have your antennae up anywhere and everywhere, and they will serve you well. All of a sudden you'll hear all the conversations going on—in your office, in the stores you visit, with your kids. You'll start to feel things. You'll start to form opinions.

I could be in one of the furniture stores I managed, and I'd know if the people working there liked it or not, if things were going well or if there were problems. It is the same thing at Starbucks. I'd listen to the walls talk every time I visited a store. I still do it today. Good managers have their antennae up. It's like they've got eyes in the backs of their heads. Good managers will sense when something isn't right with a customer, and they'll go up to the person and ask how everything is and what they can do to help.

Listening to the unspoken can be the hardest thing to do. A rule book doesn't tell you how to tune in to a customer's needs, but when your antennae are up, you can feel how your customers and colleagues are doing. You can sense good days and bad, outgoing days and quiet ones, stressful days and relaxed ones. You can sense what needs to be done.

When we were small, store meetings were Sunday night. I loved going to those meetings. We'd talk about the coffee, schedules, and changes that would make things work better. But mostly we talked about the people we served and how our jobs were a lot like being social workers. We'd talk about how we had only ten seconds or so to determine what kind of day a person at our store was having. We had just that bit of time to set aside our own needs to pay attention to their needs. If we truly believed our goal was to serve people and make a difference in their day, we couldn't follow some script from a rule book. We needed to meet *their* needs—not our own. We needed to truly listen and care.

Listening Works

Baseball fields talk just like the walls do—if you listen for it. I've read that the Mets's bench coach, Jerry Manuel, is a second set of eyes and ears to Manager Willie Randolph. His famous sixth sense for doing the right thing at the right time was awakened through his study of the great leaders Martin Luther King and Mahatma Gandhi and honed through the lessons he learned from his mentors in the game, managers Felipe Alou and Jim Leyland.

During batting practice, Manuel will find a secluded spot on the field—usually behind second base—to watch. He listens to the small talk and watches the players. He picks up any hints of information that might guide his hunches throughout a game. Manuel will also pore over the data, but he doesn't let it determine his strategy. He hears the walls talk. He pays attention. He listens, in real time, to the reality on the field. "I feel very strongly that the game has a certain flow to it," says Manuel. "You make adjustments as it goes on."

A mentor of mine from long ago instilled a similar idea in me, and it was the start of my understanding that the walls talk. I remember him telling me that almost 100 percent of people who manage a store will unlock the door to the store, walk in, flip on the light switch, head to their office, start to get things set up for the day—and do it the same way every day of their lives.

His advice, if I really wanted to get a feel for my store, was to experience my store a different way every day. If there are two doors, go in through a different door some days. Sometimes get on your hands and knees and crawl to your office. After closing or before opening, when no one else is in the store, sit in the middle of the floor and just listen. You learn so much when you see things in a fresh way and really listen. This applies not just to retail stores but to our corporate offices, too. Take a different path. See who's there, and keep your antennae up. You'll hear the walls talk.

Compassionate Emptiness

There is a quote on my office wall that challenged and frustrated me long before I was able to make practical sense out of it: "Compassionate emptiness." Like a mental hologram, this is a concept from ancient eastern religion that teaches a different approach to communication—one that is more complex, requires more energy, and demands more vulnerability.

> **To handle yourself, use your head; to handle others, use your heart.**
>
> — ELEANOR ROOSEVELT

Compassionate emptiness involves listening *with* compassion but *without* preconceived notions. Compassionate emptiness asks us to be caring but empty of opinions and advice. As the Western Buddhist teacher Joseph Goldstein explains it, "Compassion and emptiness are not two different things. Compassion is not a stance, but is the simple responsiveness to circumstances from a place of selflessness. The emptier we are of self, the more responsive we are."

Just think of compassionate emptiness in terms of husbands and wives or parents and children. A friend of mine told me about Deborah Tannen's work in this area. She's a psychologist and expert on communication who applied her thinking to mother-daughter relationships in her book *You're Wearing That?*

What she discovered is that mothers express their concern and love for their daughters by trying to improve and "help" them. Mothers seem to have a near-universal drive to correct and comment on their daughters' looks and clothes, analyzing how the daughter is taking care of herself and presenting herself to the world. In this modern form of mother love, only a mother cares enough to improve you. So why does it hurt or make daughters angry? Well, this mother communication may be compassionate, at least from one point of view, but it's not empty. And from my experience, fathers do exactly the same thing.

Compassionate emptiness levels the field. We recognize that no one is special. No one has all the answers. No one person is the leader. We are all equally thirsty.

Think about what happens when somebody comes into your office with a problem—whether work or personal. The tendency is to want to solve it. But most of the time, people aren't asking for help, they're asking to be heard. And most of the time, you shouldn't be solving the problem anyway. There's a way to help people move through their concerns without owning them yourself. That's compassionate emptiness. It's full of compassion but empty of solutions. It's very difficult to do.

Yet if you are able to grasp and harness lessons of compassionate emptiness, they will be your guide to listening and communicating in a new and profound way.

Listening Habits: Open Ears, Open Eyes, Mouth Not Flapping

The concept of compassionate emptiness gives us a tool we can use to listen and communicate with less of an agenda and more caring. It's not that we don't know how. We all know what good listening is and the techniques for healthy communication. But knowing and doing are not the same. A fresh perspective helps us tune our antennae and connect with people in more truthful and meaningful ways. Here are ways to experiment with and practice compassionate emptiness:

Do It in Person: There Is No Substitute for Human Exchange Sit down and talk with people. Take time to listen. You will learn more—and probably accomplish more—than

you would sending a dozen e-mails. Stop sending memos, and go have a cup of coffee. While technology has increased the quantity of our communication, it hasn't improved the quality of it. Not only that, it can be an obstacle to successful communication because it takes away the critical nonverbal components. Haven't we all had the tone of an e-mail completely misinterpreted? I've heard well-known leaders say that some of the worst decisions they've ever made were in a video conference. There is no substitute for true human exchange. Let people express themselves and really try to understand what they are saying and feeling instead of projecting your own ideas and needs onto the situation. Forget about the task for a moment, and think about the person. Let them know you care, and ask the question, "What can I do to help you?"

Listen for the Meaning Below the Surface One time a person on my team came to me with a problem she was having at work. As she explained her struggles and feelings, I tried to figure out what exactly was bothering her. Her emotions were soon clear to me—or at least I thought they were clear—as she began to cry. I went around the desk to give her a hug and reassure her, thinking that was what she wanted and needed from me. But I had gotten the situation all wrong. She absolutely recoiled. She wasn't sad. She was angry. She didn't want me to do anything other than listen and acknowledge the truth of the matter. She went on to tell me the issues that were causing her grief. I had to wait and let *her* tell me what she meant. True listening is creating a space for people to tell you what they mean.

> Don't be fooled by me. Don't be fooled by the face I wear.
> For I wear a thousand masks, masks that I'm afraid to
> take off, and none of them are real. Pretending is an art
> that's second nature with me, but don't be fooled. . . .
> Please listen carefully and try to hear what I'm not
> saying, what I'd like to be able to say, what for survival I
> need to say, but what I can't say.
>
> — CHARLES C. FINN, FROM "PLEASE HEAR WHAT
> I AM NOT SAYING"

Let Silence Fill the Heart You'll be amazed at the power of silence. Pay attention to how people fill it. What questions, worries, and issues do they fill it with? Their insecurity? Their confusion? A problem that has been weighing on their mind? Or see what happens when you put a topic on the table and simply ask, "How do you feel about that?" Sometimes the hardest thing to do is listen when nothing is being said. Many times people want to fill that space. Keep your ears open, your eyes open, and your mouth not flapping. Give it time. Let the silence fill itself. It may mean thirty seconds. It may mean a minute. It may be five minutes. But it will come. You get to the bottom of a lot of problems quickly by trusting the silence to reveal the heart of things.

Ask, and You Will Hear "No news is good news" is a familiar refrain, but it's not necessarily true. Nor is its corollary, no news is bad news. You can't know unless you ask. The key is to find out. If you ask, you'll learn about problems sooner, so you can fix them. And you'll hear about successes sooner, so you can run with them. If you create an atmosphere of open dialogue and communication, where everybody listens to one another and acknowledges that everybody has worth, then you are bound to get the best ideas on the table. You will find out about issues long before they become problems.

Ask, and you will hear. The goal is to encourage everyone to express their opinion. Of course, you can't act on everything, but you can certainly listen, consider, and learn. People understand that not everything will be acted on. But if you honor the opportunity to contribute, people will continue to contribute.

Recently I saw a store manager at a Starbucks meeting, and I asked her how she was doing. Well, it opened a floodgate. She was feeling bored and wasn't excited about what she was doing. I wouldn't have known if I hadn't asked. I got a chance to hear what was really going on with her and with her experience of Starbucks. If she was feeling that way, there were many more who felt the same way. I got an opportunity to learn, she helped me take action on an issue, and she got a chance to be heard and to have a sounding board for the issues she was dealing with.

Make It Safe It's amazing how few people speak up. People get their instructions, what some companies call their marching orders. We have them at Starbucks, too. Put the cups on the shelf in this way, or make the drink that way. Often a missive or a directive comes scooting down from the support center and is sent into the stores, and it turns out not to be the right thing to do. It's amazing how few people speak up.

Finally, one person stands up and asks, "Do you know this is what we're doing, and it doesn't work?" Sometimes a whole program has been implemented, and a month has gone by and one person finally stands up and says it doesn't work. The question is, Why did it take so long for someone to stand up and say something?

The reason is simple. No one felt safe enough to stand up to perceived authority. In this way, a mistake can continue for an inordinate amount of time. The fact is, most of the store managers may have been aware that it wasn't the right solution, but the typical manager's reaction is to say, "Well that's just the way they want us to do it." Whose fault is it? It's leadership's fault. I say shame on you, shame on us because we didn't make it safe enough for everybody to stand up and tell us sooner that there was something wrong with the plan. The fact is, 99 percent of the people should have felt safe enough to say something and should have been able to take that risk. They should have been able to be heard.

People are innately fearful. Most of us want to express an opinion, but too often we hold back because we're afraid. We don't want to be rejected or scorned. We don't step up and say what's on our minds. The mark of good leadership is to work hard to bring out the unsaid. You have to be relentless about getting people to say what's on their minds. You have to make it safe.

Sometimes you make it safe, and someone else doesn't. The groundwork of trust and safety you've attempted to establish may get negated by something or someone else. You always have to be on guard against factors that can break down trust and create a sense of fear. No matter how great your organization's culture is, there are always people and events that are fighting against it. But if your antennae are always up and you listen to the walls talk, you'll sense the shift in your people, and you can take some kind of corrective action.

Be Responsive None of us are too busy to respond to requests to be heard. When people in your organization reach out, they do so for a reason. You may know the person, or you may not know them. There may be a specific problem, an idea, or a complaint. If you don't take the time, if you don't tune in, you won't know. Make it a habit. If corporate chieftains of the likes of Michael Dell can answer their e-mails, all of us can. If someone from your organization calls and wants to meet or talk with you on the phone, don't say no. I can honestly say from personal experience that saying yes to people is always the right thing to do. I never say no to the people I work with. Ever. If you're tired, overbooked, or dealing with other priorities, you can find a way, even if the time needs to be delayed. Making time for people can always be done.

Give Feedback Being silent to truly hear and care can lead to great understanding. But people need feedback, too. Listening to the needs of others can also mean that you express an opinion, provide honest responses, and share information. Giving feedback can be as simple as stopping by to say hello when you notice someone you haven't seen in a while or walking down the hall to talk instead of sending an e-mail. It can mean saying, "I'm disappointed with these results," or "I'm sad and frustrated when we have to turn customers away," or "Your success thrills me!"

Commit the Time to Gain Alignment Truly trying to
listen and communicate effectively requires more face
time. People who come from other companies always
accuse Starbucks of having too many meetings. Perhaps
in some cases they are right. But that constant dialogue
gets everybody to buy in. Sometimes the process is slower,
certainly, and I've even railed at it. But at the end of the
day, when it all comes out and we get to the conclusion,
we've gained alignment.

Get to "Flow": Communicate About the Right Things
If you're not getting the answers you need, listen at a
different "frequency" or from a different angle. All artists
and scientists know that when you're working on the right
problems, there's a sense of being tuned in, and elegant
solutions will flow. When things are overly complex, you're
probably tangled in your own underwear. Perhaps you're
listening to an internal discussion about whether a product's
packaging should be red or white. Maybe the question is,
What do customers like better, red or white? Then you
know what you're listening for—and why. When you listen
to the walls talk, you pull in information, gut feelings, and
experiences that become an internal resource and compass
for decision making, direction, and guidance.

Making Listening Mistakes—Clean Up Your Messes

The biggest mistake we can make is not paying attention to
people. What better recent example is there than the exit of the
former CEO from Home Depot at the end of 2006? According

to all the articles written at the time, he didn't listen. His bottom-line, numbers-driven, Six Sigma orientation to increase profits and shareholder returns went against the customer-centric company he inherited and the needs of the people he served.

At the annual shareholders meeting before his departure, his lack of listening went so far as to exclude any outside directors from the meeting and to limit shareholders' questions. In his own comments about his performance, he said, "I used to play football. In football, you always know the score. Now it's like we are ice skating and you've got a bunch of judges on the sideline shouting out the scores." But the people he called the judges were really the jury. They were the very people he served, and he needed to be listening to his customers, employees, and shareholders. The numbers don't talk or judge or build an organization. People do.

If a person walks into your store or your office, and your mind is somewhere else, that person can see that you're not listening. We all do that. An assistant or a manager might come up to you all excited about something, but your mind is in another place. Maybe you roll your eyes, and that says to them, as though in so many words, "Can't you see I'm busy?" or "I don't have time for that now." In the moment, it's a small thing, but it can lead the person to shut down.

In fact, a whole department or organization can shut down. You had an opportunity to communicate, but you missed it. Pretty soon they won't tell you what's on their minds because they figure you're too busy or uninterested to care. If you pay attention, it's so easy to say, "I can't listen right now, I have a lot on my mind right now, but I really want to hear what you're saying. Can we talk tomorrow?"

Of course we all mess up. It's part of being human. Take it as a learning opportunity. You have to clear your mind, ask for forgiveness, and make a plan to follow up with that person to listen and gain understanding. Be assured this is a human skill that will serve you wherever you go. If your communication habits are not good at home, your habits will not be good at work.

I certainly have had my share of messes to deal with. I get emotional. I get angry, I get impatient or preoccupied. I've messed up a million times. Mouth flapping instead of ears open. But I've learned you have to deal with the mistakes and attempt to clean up right away. You have to talk to the person you ignored or hurt.

As for those times that you didn't take time to listen, the key is what you do afterward. There are no perfect communicators. There are no perfect human beings. Correcting when things aren't right is as much a part of communication as the actual act. It shows we're listening for the truth, and it shows we care.

T-Shirt Fridays

In the early days of Starbucks, we had opportunities to get together a lot. We were tight geographically, so communications could happen face-to-face.

Most of the time when we got into trouble, it was because we weren't listening to our people. In our rush to make decisions and deal with whatever issues came up in an expedient fashion, we just didn't pay enough attention to our people. We were cavalier and thought, "What do they know?" and we went ahead and did it, whatever it was. It always came back to bite us.

In one of our markets, the baristas and store managers had created dress-down Fridays. The idea was for everyone to wear whatever Starbucks T-shirts they wanted, rather than the typical polo-style shirts. Some manager or regional leader got the idea that T-shirt Fridays shouldn't continue. It came out of concern that, as we grew, there had to be more structure to ensure a standard across all our stores. But the affected people said, "Yeah, we do want T-shirt Fridays to continue." The whole issue became bigger and bigger within the organization. It became a symbol of our not listening enough and not caring enough. In our rush to deal with issues that were coming from every direction, we sometimes moved too hastily, not asking for sufficient participation and feedback from the people most affected.

The fact is, it's not possible to dictate to people what is and isn't important to them. The feelings and thoughts will still be there. At the end of the day, our actions didn't match our values. That created a problem and a distraction for us that we did not need to have. Listening, whether about T-shirts, a new business opportunity, or a breach of trust, is always important.

Open Forums

Many people have heard of Open Forums at Starbucks. They are meetings that take place all over the country, and anyone in the organization is encouraged to attend in order to communicate and learn.

We would use Open Forums to deal with changes or to bring up issues where there was conflict or potential conflict. Many times people would be afraid to air their disagreements. Often, after asking quietly about something, the answer would be silence. Store managers didn't want to be known for being negative. They thought it went against the spirit and leadership of the company. So I would bring up the issue just to make sure it got on the table.

Sometimes the silence was deafening. I had to learn to deal with that silence and let it be. If the goal was to have people involved in the dialogue it meant my mouth couldn't be flapping. A question might be raised and it might take one or two minutes for someone to speak up. Once the first person spoke, the floodgates would open, and the whole room would come alive and contribute to the forum. If we hadn't had the patience to let there be silence, I don't believe this all would have happened.

At one point, we wanted to introduce some additional beverage flavors to the Starbucks menu. At that time we had vanilla, almond, and chocolate, and maybe hazelnut. Given how the variety of drinks has grown, it's hard to imagine that there was tremendous pushback from the store managers. But at that time they were concerned that adding these items to the menu would overload the stores, making it more difficult to make drinks, and that the added options would make the menu too complex. There was also concern that the baristas wouldn't be able to keep up with the number of customers needing to be served.

In one particular Open Forum, I said, "OK, I've heard there's a lot of disagreement about adding a couple more flavors. Let's talk about it." I knew from private conversations who didn't like it, so I went on, "OK, Jim, you don't like it. Tell me why you think we shouldn't do it." We'd hear him out, I'd tell him I understood, and then I turned to another person, saying, "Mary, you don't like it. Tell me why."

What you learn over time is that by listening, by allowing people to express their opinions, and express them in public without retaliation or being looked down upon, you dissipate the fearful energy. We might not have gotten 100-percent agreement for the new flavors, but we did achieve an understanding among us. We settled on testing the additional flavors in a few places to see what happened. We came up with a way that people could get on board. We created a situation where people could talk about it more, and they could still disagree. We could all move forward because they were heard.

Open Forums became a way of life at Starbucks. New ideas came up, and bad feelings were aired. When things went wrong, we allowed one another to talk openly and honestly without any fear. Those clear channels, that culture of listening and being heard, has made a huge difference in our ability to constantly keep our organization moving forward.

It's easy to think, "I'm the president or the department head. I'm the one responsible. I'm the one who needs to make the decisions." It's tempting to demand that people simply get on board. How often are people told: "I don't want to hear your negative thoughts." There are no negative thoughts there are just thoughts. It's all positive. It's all feedback. You learn from all of it.

Listening Brings Openness and Clarity

Listening can often solve problems faster than anything else. Whenever that edge of worry about results, deadlines, conflict, or lack of direction sets in, listening can offer a new pespective and fresh solutions. Listening for the truth is a principle that can anchor you even, and especially, when you're not sure of where you're going, or what action to take, or whether there even is a right thing to do.

Listening opens doors and can create the path for you and your organization to follow.

EXTRA SHOTS: Listen for the Truth

- What do the walls say in your office, your hallways, your stores, or places where you interact with clients and customers?

- If someone came into your home and listened to the walls talk, what would they say?

- Whom have you not heard from? Whom do you need to listen to? Make a plan to meet or talk on the phone—today, this week, this month.

- How could compassionate emptiness be more at work in your conversations?

- Which listening habits do you most need to work on? Choose one or two and practice them daily. See what happens.

- Do you have a communication problem with another person that you need to take care of now? Make a plan to follow through, and stick with it.

6. BE ACCOUNTABLE

Only the Truth Sounds Like the Truth

Turn your fear into faith.

— RAY KROC

The word *truth* is loaded. Everybody has their own concept of what it means. The human experience is grounded in perception. There is telling the truth, as in not telling a lie. There is telling the truth by articulating an opinion, even if there is a risk in doing so. Then there is what I think is the purest truth: self-truth. The essence of self-truth is knowing who you are, why you're here, and acting accordingly. To me *truth* is synonymous with *accountability*.

One of the biggest mistakes leaders make is to withhold the truth and avoid accountability with their own people. Even when there is no official communication, the need for information does not go away. Something will fill the vacuum. There will be huddles in the hallways, private conversations behind closed office doors, or e-mail flurries that never do the company any good.

There's no way around it. Only the truth sounds like the truth. Plus, people are always smarter than organizations give them credit for; they can always smell a dead fish before management does. Even when it is not explicitly stated, your customers know the truth, your people in the organization know the truth, and your suppliers and business partners know the truth.

Harold Geneen, the CEO of ITT who grew an $800-million company into a $28-billion global conglomerate, demanded real facts, not details disguised as facts, in order to keep on top of his far-flung empire. In explaining his obsession with the truth, he said: "I believe it is an immutable law in business that words are words, explanations are explanations, promises are promises—but only performance is reality. Performance alone is the best measure of your confidence, competence, and courage. Only performance will give you the freedom to grow yourself."

If you're truthful and accountable to the truth, everyone around you knows. When faced with uncertainty, honesty and accountability trump everything else. Performance is the truth to measure yourself by.

Layoff Truths

When I was in one of my first significant leadership jobs, it was my responsibility to orchestrate a round of layoffs. It was one of the toughest moments in my relatively young life as a manager, so you can just imagine how I felt when I heard that a member of the management team had accidentally left the list of people to be laid off on the copy machine. I can't even describe what it felt like. I sat down and thought to myself, "Oh s_____," and then, "Oh s____" again, "I don't want to have to deal with this!" So there I was with a knot in my stomach, struggling with how to handle the situation, when my assistant looked at me and said, "Howard, only the truth sounds like the truth."

She was right. Even though ignoring the mistake and pretending it hadn't happened would have seemed much easier, I realized that the only thing I could do with a clear conscience was to tell the truth. I called a full company meeting for the next morning. We sat down in a room filled with a couple hundred people and talked about the state of the business, the situation we faced, and why we thought the layoffs were necessary. Why hide anything? We had everything to gain and nothing to lose.

Taking the nerve-racking but simple step of being honest with everyone in the company made a huge difference in the way people handled that difficult situation. What was the result of this honesty? Well, to my surprise, it was more honesty and more communication, and it made a difficult time a lot easier to deal with. Instead of people looking around for the bogeyman, they participated in the process.

I committed to daily briefings and kept people updated along the way, which helped everyone deal with how they were feeling. People can handle more than we think. We all want to know the truth, so we can make our own judgment about it. We still had to lay off those people, but they were a lot more prepared for it because we had communicated with them honestly and openly throughout the process. One person's big mistake turned out to be one of my most important business and life lessons.

In this era of ethics scandals and an environment of overall lack of trust in leadership, telling the truth—and telling it with care—becomes more important than ever. But too many times that care is missing. Recently, a leading electronics retailer, either afraid of or unwilling to deal directly with the truth, made the wrong kind of headlines when they laid off several hundred employees via e-mail. How could that possibly build trust in an organization? Such lack of care affects not only the people who are let go but all of the people who are still there, who have to wonder if they are going to be treated the same way.

The inability to deal with the truth in a straight-up way has ramifications beyond the immediate situation. A culture of caring and honesty is the backbone of an ethical and productive organization. When that culture is eroded, it can be a monumental task to rebuild it. The inescapable reality is that when a sense of caring ends, the sense of trust and shared purpose ends with it.

Language Matters

The best thing you can do to communicate clearly and honestly is to call things the way they really are. When you do speak, be sure to be real. This can be hard to do in a business world overflowing with jargon. Words like *brand, employees, assets,* and *leverage* are empty abstractions. Language really does matter. But it will seem like a silly corporate initiative, or worse, if you don't make language reflect your intent *and* put authentic, tangible actions behind it.

At Starbucks, all employees are called *partners*. Every person who works there is called a partner. One reason is because everyone who works there has the opportunity to have stock in the company. But even more, we use the term *partner* because that's how we want one another to feel and how we want to treat one another. The idea is not to fabricate an idea but to remind us that we are all partners in a collective dream.

We don't have a "headquarters," we have a "support center." This isn't something that happened when we got big; it's something that was important to us early on. In our retail business, we see our stores as the center of our universe—you can get our coffee in a lot of places, but the stores are where the service experience takes place. It's where our retail customers are, and it's where all the human interaction occurs. Everyone who is not in a store is here to support that interaction with the people we serve. We are here to support our store partners and make their lives better. When we serve one another, we enable our partners to serve others and keep us all connected to the bigger dream.

It makes me happy to see and learn from other companies who work to instill similar language and philosophy. I have nothing but respect for those who do it sincerely, because it represents who they are and what they believe, rather than repeating some hollow slogan from a book or consultant on how to create a kinder and gentler company. Don't use words to try to mask or inflate. And don't promise something you don't intend to deliver. Make sure that what you say reflects what you mean and who you really are.

Even if you haven't consciously thought about language as a way to shape the culture and identity of your organization, it's possible to start at any time, if you keep it honest and sincere and true to who you are.

The Half-Truth of Good Intentions

Most everyone starts with good intentions. We want to speak the truth to our boss, to be a change agent in the organization, to meet the real needs of the people we serve. But when we encounter conflicts within the system, we can begin to compromise.

It starts in subtle ways. We might take on a project we don't believe in, without voicing our concerns, or we might choose not to correct someone else's false assumption, because we think it makes us look good or makes our job easier. We might be intentionally vague and disguise our true meaning with jargon.

Little by little, we start compromising where we shouldn't. We stop telling the truth as we see it. We might tell half-truths to half of the people, and before we know it, we've broken trust a thousand little times. Small choices can ladder up to your demise or, even worse, an ethics problem. The fear of the truth can lead to the pain of untruth, because the truth always comes out. Untruths break down the fabric of the organization and make the cause meaningless.

Most public companies find this out sooner rather than later. At Starbucks, living up to our word is so much a part of our culture and identity that an erosion of that trust always has measurable effects. We have always believed in living up to our word, whether it's with Wall Street or Main Street.

Once, as we neared the end of the last month of a quarter, we were struggling to make our numbers. We were pretty sure we could make the outside numbers, but we were doubtful we could pay the bonuses that we felt our people deserved. To quickly improve our results and our ability to pay out bonuses, we devised a plan to tighten up our expenses.

Starbucks always gives away an extra cup, extra coffee stamps for the kids, and other similar requests. We never said no. So, seemingly out of the blue, we decided to cut back on extra cups, extra coffee stamps, even extra cleaning supplies, in an attempt to save money. And we did it without consulting with our people working in the stores every day.

We could have asked what each person could do to help tighten expenditures without doing any damage to our customer relationships. We could have gotten their support by explaining that we might not be able to pay bonuses but we were going to do the right thing.

In the end we did the opposite of what we should have: We broke trust—the heart of the work we do—and we hurt our business. We had to work hard to regain the trust we had lost.

Telling the truth is being truthful with yourself first, and then with others. Make your intention and your behavior one. There is no "truth of omission." Avoiding the truth always makes problems worse and everyone loses. When you define "telling the truth" this way, you see how high the bar really is.

Trust = Truth = Accountability

Most important business decisions are made by consensus. A group of intelligent, committed people sitting around a conference table can be a great thing, a meeting of the minds, but it can also take on a life of its own. Sometimes an idea or solution is suggested that sends the momentum of the group off in a particular direction. When that happens, even in situations in which you disagree with the consensus direction, it is easier to go with the flow and not speak up than it is to voice your opinion.

However, when the herd surrounds you and the group starts bounding down a trail that you aren't comfortable with, it's more important than ever to speak up. Perhaps others will agree, perhaps they won't, but the combination of truth, fact, genuine caring, and passion has remarkable power to move a conversation or decision.

In fact, academics who study group dynamics have determined that trust is the key ingredient that leads to positive cultures of open dissent and effective decision making. Social scientists commonly make a distinction between good decision-making groups that engage in "task conflict" and stay focused on the content of what is being debated versus bad decision-making groups that engage in "relationship conflict" and attribute disagreements to the personalities, characters, and motivations of the participants. But it turns out that these types of group conflicts are not as distinct as we might think.

In a study of seventy top management groups, two Cornell professors found that teams that engage in task conflict often experience relationship conflict as well. However, there was one factor the researchers identified that allowed groups to stay focused on the task conflict without resorting to relationship conflict. It was trust. They found that the greater the trust among participants, the more willing and able they were to push through the issues without fighting. By extension, if you want to have an honest exchange and deal with the truth, you have to create an atmosphere of trust.

In any group setting, from a team meeting to a department meeting to a companywide meeting, ask yourself, What do we stand for? What are we doing here? What do I need to contribute? Say what is bothering you, and do it often. As a mentor of mine once said, people can hire hands and heads anywhere. You're paid for your opinions. You have a voice; use it.

Work to build trust with your staff and team members. Show you care, listen, encourage independent thinking. A basis of trust will create a culture of honesty and accountability.

> **Take a minute:**
> **Look at your goals.**
> **Look at your performance.**
> **See if your behavior matches your goals.**
> —KENNETH H. BLANCHARD AND SPENCER JOHNSON,
> *The One Minute Manager*

Sustainable Trade

The bigger the company, the more it happens. You become a magnet for other people's truth and sometimes untruth. But the same dynamic holds when speaking to people outside the company. Truth and accountability are the goals and trust is the bridge that will get you there. At Starbucks that's always the starting and ending point. We use truth telling as a guide— it's our beacon when we face a challenge.

As a fast-growing, global, and highly visible company, we garner constant scrutiny, both good and bad. In the early days of dealing with questions of sustainable trade, we weren't aware of all the issues and debates. At one point, we received a letter from a group, and unfortunately we didn't respond quickly. We heard from the group again, and of course their demands increased, and things started to get heated. I remember talking to Dave Olsen, who at that time was the head of all our coffee sourcing, buying, and roasting, and we said to each other, "Why don't we just invite them in. We'll talk to them about anything. We'll share any information they want."

We set up a meeting with a couple of leaders of the organization and listened to their issues. We asked straight out, "What exactly do you want to know?" We answered all their questions openly and honestly. Some questions dealt with what we sold the coffee for. Other questions dealt with how much profit we made. We were totally transparent. Their assumption was that Starbucks tried to pay the least amount possible. That was not the truth. As we explained and demonstrated with the details we shared, our aim was, and has always been, to get the best-quality coffee. If it cost more, so be it. At the end of the conversation, we had created grounds for trust about the coffee we buy and the coffee we sell. We were able to build a relationship with an organization that could have become an adversary.

At Starbucks, there's an equilibrium that takes place. The goal isn't cheapest. That's why we've always tried to pay above minimum wage. That's why we pay for premium coffee beans. We want the most committed people who really care about what they do, and we want the highest-quality products to sell.

When individuals or groups of individuals want to confront companies with concerns of wrongdoing, lack of responsibility, or any other matter, it's easier to take aim at the company as a whole. The fact is, corporations aren't good or bad, people are. Corporations aren't honest or dishonest. People are. If you want to have an organization that speaks the truth to one another, then you better be speaking truth to everybody. That requires some vulnerability, and it requires values that are built into the organization's DNA.

Own It

There is nothing more important to me than the idea of *owning it* when *it* is the truth. No matter how much self-loathing or fear of rejection you experience, it's necessary to say, "I was wrong, I own it, I did that, it's my responsibility." But you have to do it like you mean it. The goal is not only to take responsibility for the situation, it is to show others that you can make a mistake and go on.

When poor decisions are made, it isn't someone else's fault, it's yours. You are part of the herd, too. No matter how difficult it is to do, it is important to take responsibility for the problems as well as the successes. *Me* is always *we*. The Torah says, "Thou shalt not stand idly by." We all have a part to play. When things are wrong, the leader takes the responsibility; when things are right, the leader gives credit to others.

Your Job or Your Hat?

Self-truth is the most important kind of truth. You know in your heart if you believe in your company's mission and the role you play in making it happen. You know if you trust the leadership and the people you work with every day. You know if the words your company uses match the actions of its people. If your trust in the organization or your sense of the rightness of the work you're doing isn't there, you owe it to yourself to honestly assess the situation and take steps to change it.

Whether it's out of fear or misguided priorities, if you place a higher priority on the security of your job than on telling the truth, especially to yourself, you will lose sight of your purpose and the passion that drives you and lets you do your best work. It's important to stand up to the pressure to be less than honest. Refuse to let your hat blow away. Stay focused on the truth. The minute you are bound to any other master—including the one who pays your salary—you've lost.

If you're in an environment where trust is selectively given and where fear is a constant, it is nearly impossible to do your best work. If you're always looking over your shoulder, think about the amount of time you're spending worried about the ghost that's coming after you. You can't possibly be productive. As a human being, you have enough anxiety and worry without the fear that pervades some organizations and groups.

No matter how real the fear and how great your responsibilities, when you use truth as your guide, you'll discover solutions right in front of you, and you'll believe that new opportunities are possible. You need to find ways to remember your goals and your larger purpose. That focus and self-truth will give you the strength you need to change your situation—either where you are, or where you may need to go. Look at your fear with the eyes of truth and see what you can do to break it down, break through it, or break away from it.

As we are liberated from our own fear, our presence automatically liberates others.

—NELSON MANDELA

Let Faith Replace Fear

A man was in the car with his three young children and his indulging aunt right before dinnertime. The aunt turned around in the car and gave each of the children a piece of chocolate and said, "Don't tell your mom." The man pulled the car over, turned around and said, "You can have the chocolate, but don't let it spoil your appetites. And never, ever be afraid to tell your mother anything."

When the truth is left behind, it is usually because of fear. Fear that if we are honest, we'll be rejected. When the layoff list was left in the copy machine, I wasn't just embarrassed, annoyed, and sad. I was afraid. What would people think? Would they like me less? If you can't communicate openly and honestly with your girlfriend, boyfriend, or spouse without fear, what kind of life is that? How can you possibly have a good relationship? In the same way, if you can't have open, honest communication with your colleagues, your boss, or those who run the company, what kind of life is that? How can you possibly have a good experience? How can that make a great company?

Ray Kroc, the founder of McDonald's, used to say, "Turn your fear into faith." I love that. Fear blocks the doorway to the future, the place where possibility begins. What we fear controls us. What we face frees us. Always tell the truth, even when it meets with disapproval.

EXTRA SHOTS: Be Accountable

- How well do you tell the truth to the people around you?

- Do you fudge the truth to yourself with explanations, blame, or feigning ignorance? What haven't you been honest about—to yourself? To your family and friends? To your staff and colleagues? Make a plan to deal with it.

- Is there an issue in your area or organization that has gone unaddressed? How can you get the issue out into the open so it can be dealt with?

- What words do you use to describe your work and your relationships with one another? Are these words accurate? Are there different words that would better reflect where you want to go as an organization?

- How can you create more trust in your group? On your team?

- Is there a truth you need to "own"? What steps can you take now? In the future?

- Is there fear in your life, in your organization? How can you get rid of it?

7. TAKE ACTION

Think Like a Person of Action, and Act Like a Person of Thought

Thou shalt not stand idly by . . .
—LEVITICUS 19:16

oward Schultz is an outstanding leader and a consummate entrepreneur. He is clear about what he wants, and he never gives up. He has always had persistence and great purpose. The success of Starbucks can be attributed to his spirit, his strong values, and the people he's brought into the Starbucks family. He created a culture of big goals, independent thinking, and passionate caring for one another and the people we serve.

When it comes to new products and ways to serve our customers, Howard may not always personally agree with the final decision, but once the team agrees to do something, he never says, "This will never work," or "That can't ever taste good." If we have an idea, he insists that we pursue it until it does work. It may not be the exact idea that we started out with, but with persistence we come up with something that works. When the commodity price for coffee came close to tripling in one year in 1997, he was equally passionate about continuing to get the best coffee and covering the cost another way—it's what was right, and there wasn't a choice. When our partnership with Pepsi was about to fizzle out (excuse the pun), he knew we had the right partner, so he insisted that we persist until the right beverage (Frappuccino) was developed.

Everything that works takes persistence. Music had been part of the Starbucks experience from the early days in Seattle, but persistence drove the commitment to music through the organization to make it something bigger and more creative and more satisfying than anyone imagined. He saw music as an extension of the company's one hat—the perfect complement to the art of coffee—and aligned with the mission to inspire people.

Howard Schultz persists. Things that get done are performed by people who possess that level of commitment.

> **The greatest use of life is to spend it for something that will outlast it.**
>
> — WILLIAM JAMES

Passion, Purpose, and Persistence

The success of 3M was born of failure. They started out as a mining company. When this failed, everyone—from the board of directors to their employees—would not give up. They persisted and moved away from mining corundum, a mineral used in abrasives, to developing the abrasives themselves. Their first substantial profits came about due to the persistence of a company accountant named William McKnight, who set up their first rudimentary laboratory, where "Three-M-Ite," a superior cloth abrasive, a type of sandpaper, really, was invented. This catapulted 3M from a struggling company to a huge success.

The company has continued to strive and invent for more than seventy-five years. Many of their inventions were mistakes; others seemed pointless, as was the case with their non-glue adhesive.

One of their inventors was experimenting "just to see what would happen," and he came up with a new kind of non-glue adhesive, but no one in the company could figure out how to turn it into a profitable product. A fellow 3M-er knew about the invention, and he got an idea for how it might be used. The paper scraps he used as bookmarks in his choir books were always falling out. He decided to try out the adhesive on his bookmarks. It was a perfect marriage of form (invention) and function (product). It was the freedom to persist and stick with it that led to a commercial office supply, the Post-it, that seems as essential as Scotch tape.

ON PERFORMANCE

I believe it is an immutable law in business that words are words, explanations are explanations, promises are promises—but only performance is reality. . . . Only performance will give you the freedom to grow yourself.

— HAROLD GENEEN

To Food, or Not to Food

One of my big goals at Starbucks was to get the food business growing in our stores. This was something we had tried and failed to do three or four times. Take sandwiches. When I began at Starbucks, we were in the handmade sandwich business. But they took too much time to prepare, which led to lines that were too long for the people who were coming for a cup of coffee. We got out of that business without any thought of getting back into it.

But over time, customers started asking for snacks at lunch time and suggested premade sandwiches. So we tried that approach, and again it didn't work. We couldn't make money at it, and no one was very happy with the products we came up with. It was another failed effort. We just didn't have the passion, purpose, and persistence necessary to succeed. The sandwiches were like the rest of our food business. We always had a limited menu and never quite what our customers wanted. Even our board of directors wanted to give up.

Still, we needed to satisfy our customers and of course increase our sales, and I was convinced: What goes better with a great cup of coffee than a nice little snack? There was no reason we couldn't find a way to offer high-quality coffee cake, sandwiches, cookies, or other treats to go with our premium beverages. I made a personal commitment to keep on trying.

I knew one issue in particular had undermined our success in food. It had always seemed "not important" and on the periphery; there was an overall lack of commitment. It wasn't the crown jewel that coffee was, but the opportunity was there. In looking into the food problem, I found that the person who was in charge had a lot of experience in food-service companies, but he was having trouble getting people on board with what needed to get done. He was concerned with being liked and being part of the team. He was successful in that. Everybody loved him. But he didn't have the belief that he could be successful with food on his own.

So often, when something isn't working, it's the people that are the issue. It's the fit. We had the idea of pairing the talent of the person who was an expert in the food-service business with the talent of one of our younger strategic managers who had the willingness to persevere in every challenge. I was sure they'd complement each other. However, the person with food experience couldn't deal with being teamed up with someone else, and he left to find a better fit and success in a different company.

We had to convince this young manager to take over the food business on his own. He was apprehensive. It was a big challenge, and he was worried, not only about his résumé and the status of the job in a noncoffee role, but also about the fact that other people before him had failed at it. I adamantly believed that he was right for the role, and I nominated him: "This is a great opportunity for you to get on the operating side of the business. You can really make something happen here, and you can prove your worth." He thought about it for a while—it took him about a month—and he finally said yes.

In less than a week, literally, he knew he'd made the right choice. He fell in love with the opportunity and the food business itself. I've always believed, "Do what you love, and the success will follow." Don't worry about your résumé. Just let your natural gifts shine through.

This person was driven to succeed, and he believed he would not fail. He held himself and everybody else on his team accountable. During his tenure, the food sales at Starbucks blossomed. And now food is one of our fastest growing categories.

The moral of this story is this: Get the one person—one believer, doer, early adopter—who is willing to take on the challenge and stick with it and over time, perhaps sooner rather than later, others will come on board to join in the cause. We succeeded because we pushed through in finding the right person; that person rose to the challenge and because of his belief and determination success followed. At the end of the day, it all boils down to this: "If you think you can do a thing or think you can't do a thing, you're right" (Henry Ford).

The Mazagran, aka Frappuccino, Experience

When we got the idea of creating a bottled beverage, we planned it as a joint venture with Pepsi. The first beverage was called Mazagran. It was a beverage whose name came out of the French Foreign Legion. Basically it was a sparkling coffee drink. It was an abject failure. In spite of its great coffee taste and the fact that we all loved it—and some of us thought it tasted fantastic in an ice cream float—our customers didn't. Plus we weren't selling floats, we were trying to create a bottled beverage that our customers would love. I took a bottle of it and had it encased it in one of those Plexiglas display boxes so I would always remember the lesson that it was okay to fail. So Mazagran was history, but our pursuit of the right bottled beverage for our partnership was not.

We were just starting out in our stores with Frappuccino, a blended-to-order iced coffee beverage. It had become an instant hit. So we said, "OK, why don't we do bottled Frappuccino?"

Well, bottled Frappuccino today is a billion-dollar-plus business. We could have walked away from the whole thing and said bottled beverages aren't right for Starbucks. We could have said to ourselves, "Wrong partner, wrong distribution, wrong connection with our customers."

But instead, we said, "Yes, we think there's something here," and we stayed with it. Mazagran wasn't right, Frappuccino was. Frappuccino is a continuing lesson for anyone in being purposeful, passionate, and persistent. If one thing doesn't work, go to the next. Keep going, keep taking action.

A Place of Inspiration

One of the things we don't do enough of at Starbucks, that most companies don't do enough of, is celebrate our failures. Celebration of failures leads you to not give up and to try more things. It certainly leads to more trust. People need to believe that they can make things happen and that they can try things, even if eventually they don't work out, because you never know when the one you're working on will be the one that will work.

Celebrating failures gets rid of the fear of failure. People learn to trust that they can take risks and nothing bad will happen. Not taking risks and not taking action is the thing to fight against. At Starbucks we've never played it safe. Being persistent, staying with it, even when it's not working, can lead to a breakthrough when you least expect it.

Music started out as a natural, highly personal part of the store experience. In the early days, one of our store managers, Timothy Jones, would make composite tapes at home and would bring them in to be played in the stores. Later we signed on with a professional music company to supply the music. Our customers kept asking about the songs we played and where they could buy them, so we started producing tapes and selling them.

When CDs came on the scene, we made those, too. Over a long period of years, because we were dedicated to it, music became a very important part of the aesthetic of our business. It has become part of the "third-place" experience that we've created—a place that's not home and that's not work, where you can go to relax and connect with yourself and with others. It hasn't all gone smoothly, though. It takes time and work, as well as the passion and failures that come from knowing who you are and what you're here to do. Before the iPod made music ubiquitous, we tried listening kiosks, and we tried out stations for making personal CDs. We missed our mark with those. Yet when you stay with something, you are often richly rewarded. We started releasing our own CDs from recognized artists whose sounds we love. In 2004, Ray Charles's *Genius Loves Company* became a blowout commercial and artistic hit, winning eight Grammy Awards, including Album of the Year, which was hugely gratifying for us.

Books have been another way we thought we could connect with our customers and create stores that inspire people. Our first approach was to offer the books that Oprah Winfrey had chosen for her book club. Eventually that didn't work for us, but we stayed with the commitment to reading and sharing ideas and inspiration with our customers.

We tried again with single books we thought would speak to the people we serve. When we chose *A Long Way Gone* by Ishmael Beah, the harrowing yet uplifting story of a boy soldier in Sierra Leone who found freedom in America, it was a long shot at commercial success, but we were passionate about it and supported it with pride. The book hit a nerve with us and with readers everywhere. It became a number-one best seller in bookstores across the country and sold over a hundred thousand copies in our coffee stores alone.

Magic successes come and go. Not everything works. Yet you stay with something until you prove that it's a failure or you make it a success.

We've done music, books, movies, and even the *New York Times*. All of these fit with the soul of our business—the people who work at Starbucks and the people we serve. We just keep on reinventing ourselves and hopefully always will.

We didn't do these things as marketing tactics or moneymakers, although of course we wanted to make a profit. And we didn't do them because it was easy. There were tremendous internal doubts about our purpose and focus and chance for success. But when money isn't the driving force, there are lots of things you do to make the work meaningful, to make the experience better, to serve your customers better. Music, books, movies—they all make our lives a little richer and more rewarding.

Balancing Action with Patience

In 2007, Starbucks opened about seven stores a day, or about fifty stores per week, worldwide. In the early days, it took us time to get a new market up and going, sometimes longer than we expected. Anxiety would be high, and we'd think, "Maybe this will be the city that doesn't work, that doesn't fit with Starbucks' mission." We learned that you just had to give it time. We learned that lesson over and over.

When we started out, Starbucks wasn't yet a global or even a national brand. Heck, we weren't even a local brand. We didn't really have what you'd call a customer base. Every new-market opening seemed as risky as the one before. In some cases it took years and years for a market to really take off. But we believed in our idea and in giving our partners the time and tools they needed to help them be successful.

I remember when we opened the Minneapolis market, and sales weren't even close to our expectations. We asked ourselves privately and out loud to each other, "What have we done now? Maybe Starbucks has expanded as far as it can." But we gave it more time, as we have throughout our history. We opened more stores in the area, and eventually it took hold. We hit a critical mass or tipping point and grew from there.

Of course, there's no guarantee of success. Many companies have opened multiple stores that haven't worked. In our case, it was patience that made it happen—*plus* the financial ability to stay with it. Patience can't be maintained without sufficient resources. At Starbucks, we didn't bite off more than we could chew. We never bet the company. Instead of going to multiple markets all at once with one store apiece, we focused on building each city, one at a time. It was our belief in what we were doing and the patience to see it through that, at the end of the day, made our growth possible.

"Quit Digging" Doesn't Mean "Quit"

Taking action isn't a blind pursuit. Wise action means we're guided by all our principles. We need to test and question ourselves. We can be sure that we're on the right track when our actions are guided by our principles. Wise action requires that we listen to the truth as we pursue our passion. If you are caught in the question of when to keep trying and when to cut your losses, your principles can guide you. When you're working on something and you have a sense that good things are just around the corner, keep going. When the corner seems to get farther and farther away rather than nearer and nearer, then it may be time to quit digging. Own up to what's not right, and do something about it.

Chantico was a chocolate drink that we spent months and months developing. It had a rich delicious taste, but one or two sips were really all you'd want. We had done our test marketing, but when we rolled it out to all our stores, it didn't work at all. We tried to stick with it, but it was really no use. Our customers weren't buying it. We had to quit digging. We had to let it go.

Sometimes you stay longer than you should, but "quit digging" doesn't mean "quit." It means that you stop following the path you are on because it's not working. It doesn't mean giving up; it just means changing.

The Yin and Yang of Thought and Action

The Greeks worshipped both Apollo, the god of reason, and Dionysus, the god of the activity of life. The two forces have forever been linked in a paradox: Nothing happens unless you do something, yet whatever you do needs to be thoughtfully considered.

The problem is, usually we lean toward one side or another. We either jump into the conversation without thinking or we wish we had jumped into it sooner. We either commit 100 percent to a new project right away, or we take our time weighing the costs and the benefits.

When you know who you are, you recognize your own tendencies, and you start to listen to your inner voices on both sides of the paradox. It doesn't mean you must always balance your natural style with the opposite. It means pushing yourself to move a little more in the other direction than you might naturally go.

Paying attention requires you to simply be more conscious. The ancients struggled with the balance of action and thought, and we are bound to do so as well. The point is, you have to enter the struggle. Thoughtfully.

Think like a Person of Action, and Act like a Person of Thought

My motto is, "Think like a person of action, and act like a person of thought." In some situations this means, "Feel. Think. Do." Other times it means "Feel. Do. Think." Most of the time, we want to think and then act, aim and then fire. If you're always fast to fire, you're likely to miss your shot—or get shot. If you're always waiting to fire, you're liable to miss an important opportunity.

Like the journey to find our one hat, as we learn who we are, we begin to know when to think, plan, and discuss and when to stop analyzing and take action. The principles of personal leadership—caring, listening for the truth, being accountable—all require consistent action balanced with thought and feeling.

Remember, however, without action there is no life. As Emerson said, "God will not have his work manifest by cowards."

You can't get results, you can't experience your potential, if you don't take action. If you want to have an impact, if you aspire to make a difference, then you had better start doing it. Nothing is worse than wasting your life in the false comfort of inaction.

EXTRA SHOTS: Take Action

- What keeps you from having passion, purpose, and persistence in your life and work?

- What are you about to give up on that may need a little more commitment, time, or persistence?

- How do you know when you are in a hole and are just making it deeper by your actions?

- How do you celebrate failures, for yourself and for the organization?

- Are you a more action-oriented person or a more thoughtful person? Have you monitored your tendencies recently? What happened?

- Have you reached an impasse where you need to change your approach? Use your principles to lead you to your next action.

8. FACE CHALLENGE

We Are Human Beings First

> The source of any of our unhappiness is our struggling—not what we are struggling over.
>
> — UNKNOWN

The journey we call our jobs, our careers, our lives, is just an endless series of challenges. Most of them are small, and you go through them like they're nothing. You're able to right the situation, find your way, make peace, help someone, or just do the work to get something done that needed to get done. With the challenges come the anxiety and stress—and satisfactions—that we call work and life. Our daily challenges excite us and make us feel engaged with our goals and purpose. They test us. The teach us. They make us feel connected to the people around us. Along with the worry, these challenges bring passion into our lives.

Balancing on Skates

I often think about the image of life or work as a balancing act on the blade of an ice skate. We're constantly correcting, pushing forward, and righting ourselves. Little and big challenges tilt us over a little or a lot; happy endings pull us back up. If we start getting cocky with our success, listening to our inner voice can steady us on our ride. But the point is, we're always a little out of balance.

We can be tempted to limit our risk by going more slowly or more steadily, and sometimes by hardly going at all. That's when we get stuck in a comfort zone that may end up being no comfort at all. A retreat to a comfort zone can lead to crisis, just as an unplanned risk can. We topple over when we have no momentum or when we have no direction. If we skate without skill, we'll have a much harder time staying in balance or getting back in balance. Without direction, without values, without a target, we'll have a difficult time getting where we want to go and accomplishing what we hope to accomplish.

Crisis: The Storm Before the Calm

Sometimes the stakes and challenges are higher: A child is in real trouble at school or with friends; our partner's health, job, or morale is suffering; or we're feeling stuck at work, and we're hanging in balance while we try to figure out what's wrong and how we want things to change. We may feel like our skates are flying out from under us, like we're falling with nothing to grab on to.

These challenges are not just about bad things; they're about good things we want as well. There's stress with the changes and demands we need to fulfill.

We might be making a major investment in a home, a child's college education, a new entrepreneurial enterprise, or a new relationship. There can be worry and stress in thinking about the money commitment, time commitment, or emotional commitment and how can you possibly swing it. But after the decision is made and your daughter or son comes home freshman year thrilled with the experience, or you get your first new clients, or you get past whatever you struggled with, the pain passes, and the pleasure can be appreciated. Laurence Boldt, the career-planning expert, talks about this kind of crisis as a "crisis to decide." In fact, the Greek word *krísis* means "decision." A crisis, he explains, often results when we fail to decide on a direction; a crisis compels us to make the decision to commit to a new direction.

A crisis ups the ante on why we need principles of personal and organizational leadership to guide us. A crisis demands the truth—to ourselves and to others. It demands that we know, and remind ourselves, *why* we're here, *what* we're trying to accomplish, and *where* we're headed as an individual and as an organization. When we own the truth, when we're authentic, we have a starting point for facing the choices and decisions we need to make. We're no longer drowning at sea or spinning out of control on the ice. We know where we stand, and those around us know, too.

> **There is no such thing as stressful situations, just stressful responses.**
>
> —UNKNOWN

The Worst Happens: We're Human First

You can think of the human condition as the three C's—challenges, crises, catastrophes. We take on challenges; we create crises; catastrophes befall us. Some things in life and business are catastrophes. They happen *to* us. However, how we deal with them is a measure of who we are, and the process is made easier if we have principles and values to guide our actions. Sometimes there really is no "good" on the other side. People can tell you that you'll be a stronger person or a stronger company after the crisis, but there may not always be a way to solve the problem.

When Tragedy Strikes

In the summer of 1997, Starbucks was a big company with more than thirty-five thousand partners. There were stores in the United States, Canada, Singapore, and Japan, and aggressive plans to open throughout Asia and around the world. Building the company, we had faced many, many difficulties. Some were strategic, some were operational, some were financial, and many were personal. Nothing, however, could have prepared us for the terrible tragedy that occurred that summer.

On the evening of July 6, a man came into one of our Washington, D.C., stores, just after closing at the end of the Fourth of July weekend, and opened fire, killing three of our partners. The bodies were discovered at dawn the following day by the morning supervisor. It was a botched robbery. I got the call at about three in the morning, Seattle time. It was Dean Torrenga, the senior operational leader for the D.C. area. In our worst nightmares we could never have imagined that out of a simple cup of coffee we'd face a catastrophe like this—the three young people who died and the traumatic effect this tragedy had on their families, the community, and ourselves.

I wanted to comfort the East Coast leader with words of wisdom, but no words could blunt the pain we felt. Instead of planning or solving or recommending action, we both just cried on the phone for the loss to the families and the loss to our company. At that moment, there was nothing else to do. We didn't realize it at the time, but we were also crying for the loss of our innocence. For me, my world had just stopped. These were "my kids" who had been murdered, and I immediately felt it could have literally been my kids or the kids of any of the many other families whose children, friends, and relatives were managers and baristas in our stores. Never again would it be business as usual.

Howard Schultz happened to be on the East Coast, and he got himself to D.C. within hours of the shooting. He spent time with the families, with the Starbucks people, and with the community. He didn't look over his shoulder to gauge how he should react, how he could protect himself and the company from lawsuits, or how he could hide behind spokespeople and emergency protocols. As the chairman of Starbucks, he was a human being first, and his heart went out to all the people affected. It was a pivotal moment when everyone inside and outside the organization saw what you were supposed to do no matter what: Put people first.

Often in times of crisis, people become robotic. They search for a process. They try to take action, often to avoid pain. They shut down their emotions and "go through the motions," taking care of whatever tasks need to get done in order for things to go on. Senior leaders of all organizations who have faced this kind of tragedy know that they have to be strong. They have to lead. They have to set an example.

What we did at Starbucks was simple. We were human— sadly, desperately, imperfectly human. We are always human beings first. You can never walk into your office and shut the door to the pain and violence in the world. Business is never "just business." It doesn't work that way. We can never separate our heads from our hearts.

Dealing with the Truth

Every organization can survive catastrophe if its people are open and honest and accept responsibility. In the famous Tylenol crisis of 1982, when seven people died from ingesting capsules that had been laced with cyanide, CEO James Burke understood the importance of facing the truth head-on. He didn't hesitate to speak to the public, to say exactly what he knew, and to explain the frightening reality.

It was the same way when the three young people got shot in our Starbucks store. That's when the humanity really comes out. When you follow the principles of personal leadership, you open yourself up and you can deal with anything.

What gets people into trouble is denial of the truth. When you start hiding, you stop owning the truth, and you stop holding yourself accountable. When a CEO steals, when an authority figure breaks trust, those are catastrophes for the organization, its people, and the people the organization serves—sometimes a whole community, including hundreds of thousands of stockholders and others who have placed their trust in you.

The senior leaders at Enron were supposedly great people who were committed to their families and their communities. But they lacked honesty with themselves and with one another. When the company got into such trouble that it was technically bankrupt, instead of telling the truth, they dug a deep hole. As the situation deteriorated, instead of confronting the truth of what was going on, the company collapsed in a sea of lies.

If we listen to the voices in our head that say, "Don't say anything. It will blow over. Nobody will know," we bury ourselves in fear and secrets. If we listen to the inner voice that says, "You're not to blame, it's those guys over there," we trap ourselves in delusion. If we listen to the voices that say, "Stay away; watch out for the lawsuit; the lawyers are coming," we'll miss the human response that's most needed.

You need to listen to the voice that says, "These are your values; this is who you are; this is what you stand for." This voice of truth grounds you, your team, and your organization. When leaders of organizations articulate and live their values, they drive them throughout the organization, and they become a way of being. This make it possible for everybody to know and do the right thing. People don't have to look to a rule book or a manual to guide them; they can rely on the company's beliefs and principles, and act accordingly.

Staying on Course

I believe that we all need a guidance system to help us weather the big and small storms of work and life. Everything that matters to you—your dream of a happy and fulfilling life, your work and organizational dreams, your hat—is the target. The path to get you there may change, or your target may move as you grow and reevaluate, but this path is your groove that will keep you on track.

Think about this guidance system as your autopilot, like the one a pilot has on an airplane or the helmsman has on a boat. You set the controls to your destination, but you never travel in a straight line. There are forces that affect the trajectory, like wind and turbulence and air or water currents. But the guidance system stays locked on the destination and constantly makes adjustments to stay on the path.

It's the same with people. We don't move in a straight line. We can get blown off course—by happy as well as sad and difficult events. But if we know and remember where we're going, we'll find our way. Staying on course is a skill we can learn and practice. Think about the following:

Get a Bite of Success In a crisis, we often feel lost or cut off from our usual way of doing things. We may be facing a crisis of confidence, searching for direction, or dealing with the fallout of a huge disappointment, but the feelings of anxiety, fear, and being overwhelmed are similar. Whenever I get into trouble, it's usually because I've lost touch with what I want to do. If my anxiety is high, and I want to withdraw, it's usually because I don't know what I want to accomplish, or I've lost sight of my goals. Maybe the goal was bigger than I could bite. Maybe the setback offers a new direction. Maybe I need to break it into smaller pieces to get a little success, one bite at a time. The goal is to move forward and stay focused on the bigger picture.

Own the Truth—Revisited We need to own our lives, our jobs, our failures, our mistakes, our limitations, and our successes. Instead of running away from who we are, owning it gets us on firm ground with the truth. The true leader owns the truth even before the truth is fully known.

You may have a huge deal that falls through. You may sense that your whole job is going up in smoke, or you may actually hear the words, "You're fired." If you have clear values and goals to guide you, then no matter what happens, no matter what the stimulus, they will pull you through like a strong magnet.

Set Expectations and Live by Them If something bad happens—when a huge mistake is made—we need to hold each other accountable. We need to fix the problem. But screaming and yelling doesn't work. Demeaning people doesn't work. As anyone who's been around teenagers knows, if you badger them and infantilize them, they'll just hide more.

However, if the expectations are clear and we all hold each other accountable for the results, then the desired actions will be there most of the time. If they're not, everyone will be clear about the steps needed to address the problem. Expectations and everyday accountability keep an organization on track. In a storm, these same clear expectations provide the action plan.

Don't Get Caught Up in Your Own Hype Many challenges are not born out of crisis and negative experiences, they are born of success. Good times can lead to your greatest challenges. Often, when leaders start to see themselves as invincible, they loosen up on their values and expectations.

The care that was taken with setting direction, maintaining focus, and dealing with partners and clients when the times seemed to demand it goes out the window when everything is going great. There's a mind-set that if everything you touch turns to gold then you can do anything. But your values and goals brought you your success, and losing sight of them can lead to your demise, or at least serious risks. If you pull rank, let the truth slide, and stop caring about others, what and who can you rely on when the magic falters? Be careful to stay true to who you are. Don't get caught up in the voice of hype in your own head or in the noise of the marketplace.

Put People First At Starbucks, we value people most of all, more than we value money. People have always come first, from the very beginning. People come before profits. People come before worrying about lawsuits. People come before the coffee. After all, people grow the coffee, choose the coffee, ship the coffee, roast the coffee, brew and serve the coffee—and enjoy the coffee.

Taking Care, One Person at a Time

At Starbucks the value of serving people and inspiring the human spirit was a guiding principle at the very core of the company. When I had only been at Starbucks a few months, I saw what this meant in a profound and unplanned way.

One of our store managers said he needed to talk to me about something important, and he wanted to meet with Howard

Schultz as well. I tried to take care of whatever the issue was—it was what I was hired to do—but he insisted that he needed to speak to both of us. So I set up the meeting. The day we met, I remember sitting together facing each other in Howard's office when the manager told his story. He was sick and dying. He was the first person I had met who had AIDS.

The first thing Howard said was that the company would take care of all his insurance needs, and he could stay at the company as long as he wanted to. There wasn't a moment of doubt or a moment of hesitation about whom to call to check out the right response or what the financial implications would be. The person, Jim, came first. It was a defining moment for me. From that day forward, I knew in my bones what I had known in my head before, that we would always be supported when we put people first.

Inner Strength

Life is not perfect. Oftentimes life is not sweet, and things go terribly wrong, even with our best intentions and best efforts. That's why our values and the principles of personal leadership are so important. When you know your values, you can be in terrible emotional pain—you can be swallowed up by your own failures and disappointments, you can experience the catastrophe of losing a child or of a national disaster, you can get fired or lose a deal that puts your business in jeopardy—but you'll have a proven, tested path to follow to give you direction. Your values and principles are the cup for the brew that's your life. It's how you deal with the events that makes the difference.

EXTRA SHOTS: Face Challenge

- How do you deal with the crises that cause stress and anxiety? Can you use your one hat to help you stay grounded and on course?

- If you are facing a crisis with your job or life, what steps can you take to stay true to your values? What decision(s) do you need to make? When and how will you make them?

- Does your organization have a clear purpose that will guide it during the hardest times? How can you clarify it and share it more widely?

- Is success going to your head? How can you keep that excitement and not lose your sense of humbleness so you can stay focused on your larger purpose?

9. PRACTICE LEADERSHIP

The Big Noise and the Still, Small Voice

Big noise on stairs. Nobody coming down.

— CHINESE SAYING

It's easy to worship personalities—sports stars, movie stars . . . even business stars. Around the halls of most companies, you'll hear talk of a kind of celebrity: "the Leadership" or "the Management." These folks seem one part human and one part divine (or evil). But once you have been in those senior leadership roles, you realize that leaders are just like anybody else. Sometimes just a little luckier.

The relationship between a company's leaders and the people who work with them is a crucial one, yet there is often a real disconnect between the two. It's easy for the Leaders to get caught up with the "big picture" and lose sight of what—or who—makes that big picture happen. At the same time, people can be intimidated by leaders and fail to communicate well with them. Developing personal leadership means each of us at every level of an organization has the ability and the responsibility to lead themselves with integrity and to practice those principles that will serve as guardrails for honoring oneself and leading and serving others.

Big Noise on Stairs, Nobody Coming Down

Our culture admires celebrity, credentials, and executives who act like cowboys and cowgirls, expecting us to trust them implicitly because they have the "answers." We are enamored with the leaders who seem to be big thinkers. We elevate the educated and are constantly searching for experts in one field or another. We court the celebrity leaders and spokespeople and even entertainers for the glow we feel they bring to us and our colleagues.

We boost our confidence by endorsing cowboy-style leadership, which we can think of as the "my way or the highway" approach to managing people and business. *Leadership* is not a synonym for "believe me," "trust me," or, in the political arena, "stay the course." All these qualities are about creating noise on the national stage or simply having a big impact in our workplace conference rooms and boardrooms. It's become common to refer to young business leaders as "rock stars."

All these qualities have their place, but those I admire most are leaders who are big lovers. When people can think and lead with heart, then I turn my head. Big lovers are more than just passionate. They also have the ability to turn down the noise and reflect in order to generate the best and wisest solutions.

This sometimes quieter leadership is about being genuine, caring, and true to one's goals and values. The primary role of leaders is not to wow with winning ideas, but to make sure the organization lives up to its principles and dreams.

For me the Chinese proverb, "Big noise on stairs, nobody coming down," captures the complexity of personal leadership. It tells us three things:

1. Noise is just noise. It doesn't count for anything. You have to have substance.
2. It is the quieter voice, the voice of purpose, the voice of caring that matters.
3. Leaders are human beings like everyone else. Don't forget your own humanity. Don't forget the humanity of everyone around you.

Servant Leadership

I don't like requiring things because I don't like rules, but at Starbucks I strongly encourage reading a little orange pamphlet called *The Servant as Leader*, by Robert Greenleaf. It's a short treatise on the notion that the person who is a servant of all is the most capable leader.

Greenleaf does a great job talking about the heart. "One does not awake each morning with the compulsion to reinvent the wheel. But if one is *servant*, either leader or follower, one is always searching, listening, expecting that a better wheel for these times is in the making. It may emerge any day. Any one may find it out of his own experience." The servant leader understands that big noises are not as important as big hearts.

Passion can deceive. Like a football player getting worked up before a game, we can get so hyped with our self-made enthusiasm that we can't settle into our "game mind" to focus on the current reality. Just as we need to balance action and thought, so too we need to balance our passionate drive with our quiet mind. Passion can take you out of the present; we can get so hyped up with our emotions and reactions that we override our ability to really be present and "in the now." Time-outs are necessary in business, just as they are on the field and at home with our children and partners, and any time we truly care. Those who work to get beyond the big noise have the ability to turn down the volume and reflect, which generates the best and wisest solutions.

Help Groups Listen to Their "Little Voice"

When everything seems to be going right, with big profits, great headlines, and lots of positive buzz among customers, it can be hard to lead from that quiet place. It's easy to get caught up in the growth and the noise and lose track of the values that are at the root of your success.

We could feel this starting to happen at a time when we were in the midst of a gigantic growth phase. We were establishing Starbucks stores in multiple international markets, and we had expanded the distribution of our coffee beans into grocery stores. Our licensing business was growing, and we were expanding into new areas. In addition, more and more competitors were popping up. As much as we were proud of helping create the premium coffee category—at least in the United States—it was becoming an increasingly crowded marketplace. So on the one hand, we were starting to believe our own hype, and on the other, we had fears that all we had created could suddenly disappear.

As Howard Schultz has done from the very beginning through today, he challenged us to go back to our roots to understand what was most important and true about what we had created and continued to create at Starbucks. He challenged us to look at all our activities and decisions to see if our actions matched our values and our goals.

We created a several-months-long process with people throughout the organization in order to connect to our own quiet voice. We used this time to clarify and confirm the threads that drew us together. What is it exactly that a trip to Starbucks represents to the people we serve? What is it about working here that makes it special?

We discovered, or rediscovered, really, that Starbucks represents "your place"—a place to get a cup of coffee your way; a place for the people who work there to be of service in their way; a place for friendly, romantic, business, or political conversation; a place to work, think, read, or simply be with yourself. Ultimately, Starbucks is and was a place where people can come and sit and reflect on a rainy Saturday afternoon. A place for our customers to listen for their still, small voice. Not the Big Noise.

Workplaces are, ironically, full of noise. We've got the large egos of people trying to succeed and make a difference. We've got the noise in our heads—all those inner voices telling us how to be, what to do, and what not to do. Our bosses become celebrities in our Monday-to-Friday lives. It's easy to confuse noise with substance—especially our own big noise. When your ego is clamoring, "Pay attention to me," you need to work hard to see it for what it is: noise. Wherever the big noise comes from, it can keep you from hearing the truth; it can keep you from hearing the substance of what's really going on and what really needs to be done.

The big noise—the public or inner celebrity that has such a powerful hold over us—is something that we actually create. It's our imagination (the image maker) that creates celebrity, not reality. A big noise may be coming down the stairs, but it is an image we've created in our own mind. Listen for your own big noise. It's that big noise that can get you into trouble.

Change Your Place of Worship

Contrary to what you may think, good executives don't want to be worshipped. When someone shakes in their boots in your presence, one suspects the person isn't wearing one hat. What good leaders want are people who can contribute their true, creative selves to the organization. They want thought, action, truth, and genuine caring.

Parents spend a good chunk of their energy convincing their children they are unique and special, but the reality is that we are more ordinary than we are special. In fact, it's a huge release to realize we are all a lot more like each other than our roles sometimes make us believe. When we let others be ordinary, not leaders to be feared or workers to be managed, we can also be ourselves. We don't have to work at creating big noises. We can have open and authentic conversations with each other. We can partner with others. We can forgive them. We can celebrate their accomplishments. We can just be human.

What people in "authority" believe matters less than the true authority that comes from believing in your purpose, your personal vision. When you wear your one hat, you no longer will worship celebrity. Instead, you will admire people and notice people who do special or extraordinary things even when there's no personal benefit.

Pay Attention to Who Is Really Coming Down the Stairs

An organization chart outside my office got a lot of attention. I've seen this chart in lots of other companies but it's amazing how easy it is to ignore its meaning. It takes the typical pyramid and turns it upside down to look like a V. At the top of the chart are the people we serve, in the middle are the people who work at Starbucks, and at the bottom is the leadership, the bosses. It reminds everyone who enters my office that we are ultimately here first to serve one another and ultimately to serve the people who come into our stores. You don't work for the leadership. All of us work to serve others.

Here's what we need to remember:

Leaders Listen to and Serve All the People You need to listen to and engage yourself with all the people you serve, not just the 10 or 20 percent who tell you what a wonderful human being you are.

In any organization, big or small, you can think of 10 or 20 percent of the people as Pollyannas who never see anything wrong. Those are the voices that tell you what a great person you are and how everybody loves you. Then, of course, there are another 10 or 20 percent who are naysayers, telling you that you're a bum and nothing you ever do is ever right. They harbor the attitude that the leaders are wrong and that the people running the company don't care about anybody but themselves.

If the Pollyannas catch the CEO taking money out of the till, backdating stock options, or whatever the latest betrayal is, they say, No, he didn't do it, and if he did do it, he didn't do anything wrong, it was all a misunderstanding. For the naysayers, it's just the opposite. If they discover the CEO doing something unequivocally good, for instance putting every employee's child through Harvard, the naysayers will say, He's not doing it for the right reasons, he's only doing it for the press.

Then there is the middle 60 or 80 percent, the independents, who float toward one side or the other, depending on their mood and the mood of the organization.

Many leaders think they need to get rid of the negative voices. The naysayers, they believe, sound the death knell of a healthy organization and a positive environment. Not true! We need those voices. They constantly remind us and help us identify things that need to change—in ourselves and in our organization. The key is not to let those negative voices take control; we need to involve them in the organization and make them productive.

On the other side of the coin, we also need the Pollyannas. We need the people who are always telling us that things are OK, that things will get better, and that we can handle whatever is in front of us and coming down the mountain.

The fact is, we need all the voices, including the stabilizing effect of the solid middle, who hear and process the big noises—the big whines and the big cheerleading— and help anchor it in the day-to-day reality.

We need all the voices to do the best work (including all the conflicting voices we carry around in our own heads). Great leaders—team leaders, CEOs, coaches—take all these conflicting conversations, all those disparate voices, and bring them together for the productive good. They let all the voices be heard, they hear the truth, and they help everyone move forward.

Companies Can Make Big Noises and No One Comes Down the Stairs When companies make promises about who they are and what they stand for, their actions speak louder than their words. It's easy to say, "The customer comes first," or "Our people are our greatest asset," or "We care about the environment." When leaders at Starbucks say they serve the customer, everything they do better reflect that. To be successful, everyone in the organization needs to understand and share that commitment.

Starbucks stores open at a particular hour in the morning, but the partners need to be there and ready a few minutes before. We can't promise to create a meaningful moment in someone's day and then fall short. It's not easy doing it day in and day out—to keep the passion for the little things that separate the good from the great—but it is still so, so important.

Leaders Get Paid to Know, and Even When They Don't Know, They Get Paid to Know If you are leading, you are responsible. When a leader takes on a big challenge, there's a Big Noise inside, saying, You've got the goods, and you can do what is required. But the leader has to listen to the small voice inside that says, Hey, bub, they've given you a title, and they're paying you money, but you've a got a lot to learn. You'd better pay attention and listen to the people you're serving. You'd better learn from them. You'd better remember not only the things you've done right but also all the things you've done wrong, so they stay in front of you.

When I took on the role of president of Starbucks International, what the heck did I know about being president of an international company? Nothing. I had traveled overseas in the furniture business, so I had some general exposure to doing business in foreign markets. I knew about what had and hadn't worked at Starbucks. But I had no idea what would or wouldn't work in a Starbucks in the Philippines, in Korea, or even in the UK. I had to listen and learn from our operating partners. As a team, we had to learn and adapt while staying true to our hat.

In our store openings in Japan, our first market outside North America, I was very concerned with adapting to the local culture and not forcing our Starbucks ways, and our American ways, on the people we hoped to serve. I wanted to welcome our new customers with open arms and a big yes.

The question of smoking was a huge issue. From its very first days, Starbucks had banned smoking in all its stores. The smoke interfered with the coffee aroma in the store and affected the roasted beans in the bins we kept open near the counter. But in Japan, smoking was everywhere; it was part of the human exchange we wanted to inspire and celebrate.

I made the decision to allow smoking in a special upstairs section we created in our first location, which we outfitted with a humongous air exchanger. Howard Schultz was adamantly against the smoking policy, and our operating partners were so excited about the Starbucks mission, and all that they had learned while training in Seattle, that they also felt we could prohibit smoking. I listened to all the voices, but I knew there was no right answer. I carried forward with the upstairs smoking arrangement.

Well, opening day came. Everything went off without a hitch, including the coffee drinks and the carry-out service, previously unknown in Japan, and we had all the customers we needed. When the second store opened sometime later, we also allowed smoking. But by the time the third store opened, we saw that smoking sections weren't the reason people came to Starbucks; they came for the whole experience. I learned, listened, and changed my thinking—of course, with a gentle push from Howard. (Did I say gentle?) From then on, for the rest of our expansion into Japan and in every market thereafter, the no-smoking experience has become synonymous with the Starbucks experience.

Whatever your challenge, the company is paying you to know. If you don't know, they are still paying you to know—so you'd better learn.

There's a deeper lesson to knowing and learning, which was crystallized in my mind when I had a conversation with someone who worked in a company where I served on the board. The person raised the question of how much I got paid for being on that board. My answer, a bit tongue in cheek, was as follows: "You know, if you only want the knowledge I gained by all the things I did right, that comes very cheap. I'll work for ten cents on the dollar. But if you want the value of every mistake I made, that costs money. That's where the value is."

When you go to work for a company, they're paying you for all your successes. Like everyone, you think you have to put on your résumé all the things you've done right. But wouldn't there be a lot more value on a résumé if it listed all the things you'd done wrong and what you learned from those failures? The valuable experience is in the pain you've suffered, not in the trophies you've won.

Just as you need to be constantly learning as a leader, so, too, you want to hire people who can learn. Experience and skills are necessary and a given, but if I had to choose, I'd take the person who can learn over the person who knows. Hiring people who know there are rocks in the river, even if they don't know where they are but are willing to find out, is the key.

Leaders Serve When They Stay with People, and Also When They Help People Move On. It's easy to hire, but it's much harder to develop. If you want to ensure the success of your organization, you need to put the same care and attention, the same passion and persistence, the same focus and action, into the people you hire as you do into the strategy and results of the organization. If you want to grow your organization, you have to grow your people first. If you want to stick with it and grow as a company, you have to stick with the people that will grow it.

Leading others demands the most of us. It demands all the skills of personal leadership. You have to care—like you really mean it. You have to listen for *their* truth. You have

> **The best minute spent is one I invest in people.**
> —KENNETH H. BLANCHARD AND SPENCER JOHNSON,
> *The One Minute Manager*

to be accountable to the people around you. And most of all, you have to show up and be there.

Annual reviews are worthless for just that reason. They aren't about being there. Developing people requires attention and conversation every day. Get to know your people, and stick with them equally, but in ways that they need.

Great leaders don't wait for people to come to them. They go to them. Some people need pats on the back, some need constant pats on the tush. Some people are going to be quiet about what they need, and some are going to be noisy. Some people are high maintenance and others will be self-sufficient. Sticking with people means dealing with their different emotional needs, intellectual needs, and communication needs. When we don't meet those needs, we're not meeting our commitment to our people and our commitment to our organization.

When we bring someone on board, we're hiring a human being, not an asset, and with that comes all things human. Remember, we're not hiring people for the trophies they've won, we're hiring them for their potential. People often fail after getting promoted simply because the people who promoted them don't stay with them. The first time I became a VP, I certainly wasn't VP material. It took years of learning and coaching to be good at the position.

On the other hand, if someone isn't doing their job or doesn't have the desire, skills, or fit for the work before them, there's no time like now to deal with it in a direct and caring way. If someone commits to doing something and doesn't get it done, you can bet I am there. I'm direct, and I'm driven to get results. At the end of the day, for me, performance always matters, and I'm ferocious about it. I never found caring and results to be in conflict with each other. You can be nice, you can be supportive, and yet you can also be direct and demanding.

I believe if you commit to something, you're committing to the whole organization, not just to your boss. I have a little motto I try to live by: "If you don't produce results once, shame on you; twice, shame on me." In essence, what this means is that I'll take the responsibility for you the first time, but the second time you own it. As far as I'm concerned, a deal is a deal. Leadership means helping, guiding, and providing resources. Personal leadership means dealing with the truth, owning it, and being responsible for what you know *and* what you don't know.

As leaders we serve when we develop new leaders and give them the support and resources they need—in the way that they need them. We also serve when we help people move on and find places where they can be successful. It you've given it all you've got, if the person has given what they can, and they still are not achieving the expected results, then an honest conversation and an honest decision is best. It doesn't mean you're bad or that they're bad. Maybe there just wasn't a good fit, or the circumstances changed. It's not a question of right or wrong, caring or not, it's a question of being true to our one hat, where we want to go, and the best way to get there.

> Master bridge builders are ideal teachers who use themselves as bridges over which they invite their students to cross, then, having facilitated their crossing, joyfully collapse, encouraging them to create bridges of their own.
>
> — HOWARD BEHAR, PARAPHRASING LEO BUSCAGLIA

It's Not Rocket Science, It's a Lot Harder

Dave Olsen, the original head of coffee at Starbucks, likes to tell a wonderful story he heard on National Public Radio that relates to the challenges of leading and developing people.

The reporter had recently done a story where the interviewee made a seemingly unremarkable quip in talking about his experience. The person said, "It wasn't that big a deal, it wasn't rocket science."

Something about that line caught the reporter's imagination, and when he had a chance to visit a jet propulsion laboratory not long afterward, he decided to investigate its meaning. In talking with one of the scientists, he posed the question, "What do you people think of when you come up against a problem you can't quite figure out but you think you will, or should, be able to solve? You can't say it's not rocket science, since you're the rocket scientists." It turns out that what they say to themselves is, "At least it's not brain surgery."

So the reporter paid a visit to the brain surgeons at Johns Hopkins and asked them the same question. After thinking for a while, the doctors came back with their response, "At least it's not nuclear physics." So of course the reporter was compelled to talk with the nuclear scientists at some other premier institution. The nuclear physicists were pretty disdainful of the question, but after concentrating on it for a while, they explained that what they say to themselves is, "At least it's not social science." To underline the point of the whole story, social science may not seem like a "hard" science, but trying to understand the human condition is certainly a lot "harder" and a lot more baffling than trying to understand the workings of rocket science.

Dave Olsen particularly identifies with this story not because of his high-level technical expertise (though the level of his coffee expertise is pretty rarified) but because of its insight into the complexity of people. As romantic, admired, and even daunting as his coffee role was for so many years, when he made the transition to the people side of the leadership team, he realized that his coffee role wasn't nearly as difficult a responsibility as dealing with and growing people. As he explains, "With coffee, everything matters, from where it is grown, how it is processed, shipped, roasted and blended, packaged and delivered, right to the cup. But once you buy it and do all the other steps right, it's yours when you need it. With people, everything matters, too, but the investments are often less tangible, and the investment never ends." With people, you're never done. Yet most of the time, when you invest in people the rewards are great.

Organizations that focus on the *performance cycle,* defining outcomes and the steps to achieve them, without focusing on a companion *culture cycle,* will find that their results are undermined by the actions, and inactions, of their people. Leaders—with both a small and capital *l*—need to understand this investment in culture, in people, to bring out the best in themselves, their partners, and to achieve the goals everyone aspires to.

Leading Never Stops

Personal success and organizational success are not entitlements; they have to be earned every day. Reaching the big goals, keeping our eye on our own Big Hairy Audacious Goals, is achieved through daily actions in the here and now. The Big Noises create energy and passion and sometimes the confidence—or chutzpa—we need to keep going. But the still, small voice is the one that will really get us there. If you listen to that voice—in yourself, in the people you lead, in the customers you serve, and in the partners you work with—you'll stay close to your values and to what matters most to you and the rest of the organization. If you listen to that small voice, you will develop the habits of the servant leader, who is the best leader of all.

EXTRA SHOTS: Practice Leadership

- How do you practice quiet leadership? How can you make it easier for people to deal with you as a human being and not as a job title?

- How would you measure yourself on a scale of 1) Big Noise versus substance, 2) Helping others listen to their voice, 3) Listening to your own small, inner voice?

- Do you know what your people need most from you? How are you not meeting their needs, and how could you better meet them? If you don't know, ask and find out.

- Who has disappointed you or not met their commitments? Can you speak to that person today? Tomorrow? Take action, with care, and see how it feels and what it leads to.

- Can you serve more and lead less? Is there a particular person whom you could serve this week?

10. DARE TO DREAM

Say Yes, the Most Powerful Word in the World

I dream of things that are not and ask why not.
— ROBERT F. KENNEDY

Many people believe that *no* is the most powerful word in the world. As we grow up, people in power, such as our parents, our teachers, and our bosses, tell us no. "No, don't touch that." "No, you can't do that." "No, I don't have time for you right now." We grow up longing to exercise that most powerful word and to tell others what *they* can't do. As soon as we get in a position of authority, we start making up our own ways to say no.

But those who think *no* is the most powerful word are missing something. *Yes* is the most powerful word. Yes is freeing and inspiring. It means permission. It means possibility. It means you give yourself and others the chance to dream. Saying yes makes you feel good.

Getting Past the "No Book"

Once you begin saying no to one thing, you begin saying no to a lot of things. Sometimes we say no to people and don't even realize it has just become a habit.

There was a time when some Starbucks stores put up signs that said: WE DON'T ACCEPT $100 BILLS. It was the sort of notice people are used to seeing in all kinds of stores, so probably no one gave it too much thought. There are, of course, security issues when you take them, from counterfeit bills to just needing more cash in the till in order to make change. For those reasons, some of our people decided to make it easier for themselves by not accepting the large bill. But there were people we served who asked why not. When we looked at it from the customer's point of view, the sign was about us and about saying no, not about human connection and great service for every person. We realized we could say yes, and now we proudly accept hundred-dollar bills.

There was another everyday no that we turned into a yes. When a customer bangs on the door early in the morning before the official store opening, the message he or she gets is, "No, we're not open yet," or even a shout, saying, "Can't you read the sign?" We started opening our stores ten minutes before the posted time as a way to say yes to customers even before they placed their order.

All of us find so many ways to say no and put up roadblocks. Eventually, in an organization, these roadblocks find their way into an unwritten No Book, which is part of the Rule Book. We start looking for other things to say no about. People start thinking about serving themselves and not doing things that might mean taking a risk or creating more work for themselves. It's like a parent or grandparent who constantly worries that the grandkids will knock over the vase. It's much better to do the work and move the vase out of reach of those little hands. Take away the impediment, take away the no; and the whole encounter, the whole relationship, changes.

> **Don't ask what the world needs. Ask what makes you come alive, and go do it. Because what the world needs is people who have come alive.**
> — HOWARD THURMAN, PHILOSOPHER, THEOLOGIAN, AND CIVIL RIGHTS LEADER

Saying Yes Is a Leap of Faith

Sometimes saying yes can seem like a real struggle. We all know what it feels like to get dragged into agreeing to do something we think we don't want to do. There are times when we can't say yes. For example, we don't say yes to a fifteen-year-old's request for a party without chaperones, or to a significant new commitment when we already have too much on our plate, or to absolutely any action that goes against our personal values, purpose, or ethics. But we can say yes a lot more than we do. If you start finding ways to say yes as a matter of practice, you find out it is not really very hard.

Some people finally decide to get married by saying yes to the possibilities instead of no to all the things that will be different. Saying yes is something most people really want to do. Someone I used to work with once told me, "There are a million reasons to say no, but we just need one reason to say yes." Try saying yes. It can change the world.

"Have It the Way You Like It"

Saying yes is all about people. It's an emotional word that leads to actions and reactions that have emotional results.

In 1989, when I arrived at Starbucks, the company was devoted to serving great coffee and creating an inspiring place for all its customers and partners. But there were blind spots where we were saying no without realizing the impact we were having on the people we served.

Our customers had come to depend on us every day as a place they could trust to get a great cup of coffee. Some customers even started making requests for things they would like us to serve, like more tailored drinks, including specialty drinks with different flavors, a variety of milks, and noncoffee ingredients.

For a long time, Starbucks had resisted these requests. We prided ourselves on being coffee purists and felt that in order to remain successful, the company should focus on what it knew best. Some of my best battles with Howard Schultz were fought over these coffee questions, which to me as a newcomer seemed like coffee rules. I was against rules that limited what we could do to serve our customers, and I had brought my own Golden Rule with me: If it's not illegal, immoral, or unethical, and as long as we won't poison somebody and someone wants it, then we ought to try it. People should be able to have their drink the way they want it.

I didn't see how it could be untrue to our mission or the quality of our coffee if we said yes to the people we served.

Our customers were telling us what they wanted. Why were we arrogantly saying no? If nonfat milk wasn't, in our opinion, as tasty as whole milk, was that a choice we should make for our customers? If our customers wanted a latte with a little vanilla flavoring, how could that spoil our coffee?

As an organization, it was our responsibility to figure out *how* to do it. As to flavored coffee, we could say yes to adding flavors to the brewed coffee rather than adding flavor to the beans, which would spoil the roasting and aroma in our stores. Later, with food, saying yes meant not giving up on the requests we had for lunch choices and breakfast offerings. If we weren't going to have grills, then we had to figure out the equipment, sources, and combinations that would serve our customers in a consistent and satisfying way.

Eventually we decided to make changes to our operations to accommodate a much broader variety of drinks, and we invited our baristas to "Just Say Yes," with love in their hearts, to customers and to each other.

Now everyone enjoys the variety of drinks Starbucks offers and the fact that they can customize them almost any way they want. We have signs posted that encourage people to HAVE IT THE WAY YOU LIKE IT. There are so few places to be in control in one's life—why not at Starbucks? Here our customers can have—or invent—what they want. It's a small thing, but with big implications for their day.

Saying yes means giving yourself and others the chance to dream. It means taking a risk. It means giving trust. It means having faith and finding hope. If you don't believe *yes* can change the way you feel or act, try this little experiment: Close your eyes and say the word *no* ten times over. How do you feel? Do you feel a constriction in your chest? Maybe even a little tense?

Now take another breath and do the same thing with the word *yes*. Isn't that a different feeling? Do you feel yourself expand and lighten? Some people recommend that you smile before you make a call or pick up a ringing phone. It's the same idea. Saying yes opens doors—for us and others.

Leading is not about saying no. *No* only appears to be a shortcut to leadership. True leadership is saying yes to people, affirming them, giving them resources, your trust, and clear purpose.

> **Go placidly amid the noise and the haste and remember what peace there may be in silence. As far as possible without surrender, be on good terms with all persons.**
> — MAX EHRMANN, FROM *Desiderata*

Dare to Dream
The ability to "dream of things that are not and ask, 'why not?'" is the most basic and primal of human motivations. What Starbucks has become and how it happened is a bigger

dream than most of us could have imagined, and it is a dream that continues to come true for all of us who are part of the organization.

We wanted first and foremost to create a business that reflected our values and that served the communities we were part of. We also wanted to source, roast, and serve the finest coffee in the world and do it in an environment where people supported one another. We believed, and still believe, in our core mission and purpose. People are not employees but partners in the truest sense of the word. We need to genuinely care for each other, and we need to remain committed to treating others with respect and dignity. We want our values to come alive in our work, and we want to create a place where all persons can be true to themselves and their own values. We always believed that sales results and profits would come from that commitment.

Yes Takes a Leap of Faith

Saying yes takes both a belief in yourself and a leap of faith. Think of it as a leadership skill like all the others. It takes just as much practice, if not more.

It's all too easy for the power of no to take over our minds and our thinking. Like children, when we say no, we feel that rush of momentary clarity. Saying no is necessary at times, but it's not a strategy for life or business success. When we say, "Yes, I will," or "Yes, I do," we take a step toward knowing who we are and where we're going. We test out our one hat.

When we find a way to say, "Yes, I'll do it," "Yes, I'll take that road," or "Yes, I'll put my heart into that endeavor," we discover our strengths, and we find out if our goals and actions are aligned. Saying yes to our values actually gives us the strength we need to overcome our fears and face the challenges that may be in store, whatever obstacles might get in the way.

Saying yes to our one hat and our principles gives us the self-confidence and guidance we need to think independently, to show we care, and to be accountable to ourselves and everyone around us. Saying yes to people builds trust, which is the foundation of true leadership.

Saying yes means putting faith into our hopes and dreams. Nothing is more important. When we nurture and inspire the human spirit, we say yes to the world.

EXTRA SHOTS: Dare to Dream

- Are there certain people who make you think yes more than no? Who are they, and why is that?

- Who on your team needs a yes now? Do they have your trust? Can you give it?

- Consider a current problem where solutions have been rejected or seem inadequate. Can you look at it differently, so that you can say yes? Can you bring in others, listen to others to frame the problem, or offer solutions that you might say yes to?

- Can you say yes and really mean it? Regarding your relationship? A company decision? A customer?

- If you could "Just Say Yes" to something in your life now, what would be different? What do you need to say yes to yourself for today?

Acknowledgments

The seeds for this book were planted a long time ago and are tended to this day by my ongoing experiences and life lessons, and by the many people I continue to learn from. This book only exists because of the openness and commitment, the hearts and souls of the people in my life. In this spirit, I wish to express my deepest thanks and gratitude:

To Lynn Behar, my wife and life partner of thirty-two years, who helped me to understand that independence and love are not in conflict with each other. They go together and in so doing make for a partnership that is built to last. Thank you Lynn for all of your support during the journey of our life and the journey of this book. You have been there the whole way with your thoughts, editing, contributions, and, most of all, your love.

To Marvin Behar, my brother, who taught me what personal responsibility and persistence really mean; Beverly Schoenfeld, my sister, who has always believed in me and encouraged me to be all that I could be; and Ken Schoenfeld, my brother-in-law, who taught me how to work and the importance of living up to one's commitments.

To Scott and Sarina, our children, and Kim and Michael, their partners, who helped me learn that listening is always more important than having the answers; to my grandkids, Sydney, Ella, Zoey, and Mathew, who are constant reminders of the importance of energy and persistence in all that we do; and my mom and dad, Jennie and Albert, who in their lifetimes showed me what can be done with just a dream and a little hard work and who taught me the importance of family and the happiness of a simple life.

To Sid Schectman, for mentoring me like a father and trusting me with my first leadership role; Jim Jensen, who taught me about the magic of believing in myself and others and who opened the doors to a life of personal growth; Jack Rodgers, without you I would only have been a Starbucks customer; and Jeff Brotman, thank you for helping me to see the greatest opportunity of my life.

To Orin Smith, who was always there to listen, support, and make us all better through his calmness, thoughtfulness, and caring. You were always the stability in my wavering sands.

To Kathy Lewis, who has the patience of an angel in managing me and my schedule when there is more on it than I can possibly accomplish, and Dave Olsen, my friend, who I thank for being so supportive and for contributing your knowledge and your passion. You are what Starbucks is all about.

To Howard Schultz, without whom this journey of a lifetime would not have been possible. You shared your dream and your passion. You gave me permission to be myself. You encouraged me to take risks and to lead with caring and love. Thank you, Howard, for showing the kind of courage and compassion that most leaders never do.

To my friends and colleagues, who provided interviews, helpful conversations and comments, and who read portions of the manuscript, a huge thank-you for being available and for adding so much value to this endeavor. Your combined energy lives on every page of this book. Starbucks is lucky to have or to have had you all as part of the leadership team. Thank you most of all for your friendship: Jim Alling, Troy Alstead, Jennifer Ames-Karreman, Nancy Bennett, Michele Gass, Deborah Hauck, Dan Hurdle, Kathie Lindermann, Roly Morris, Veronica Park, Dean Torrenga, Paul Twohig, Deidra Wager, and Jinlong Wang.

To Annette Moser-Wellman and Jane Melvin, to whom I give special thanks as my two friends who made this book come to life through their belief in the value of the message, through their never ending nagging, and for all their initial work to make it happen. Without you I would have just picked up anchor and set sail without ever experiencing this wonderful challenge.

To Janet Goldstein, who, with passion and heart, took my thoughts and ideas and was somehow able to get them down on these pages. Through your skill, patience, and incredible coaching and perseverance, this project got done. Thanks for being the professional you are and most of all for being my friend and my partner. And thanks to her family, Andrés, Anna, and Sophia, for sharing Janet with me during our tight writing and editing schedule. Thanks also to Janet's able assistant, Karen Hatch, who did whatever was needed to keep us moving in the right direction.

To Adrian Zackheim, Jeffery Krames, Courtney Young, Will Weisser, Courtney Nobile, and the whole team at Portfolio. Thank you for taking a chance on me and this book. I hope it hugely exceeds all of your expectations. And as my mother would say, Kineahora, or so it should be.

Finally, to all of the people at Starbucks, past, present, and future. You are the ones who really made this book possible. The fact is, I was a customer for seventeen years before I went to work at Starbucks. The first cup of coffee I ever had was Ethiopia Sidamo and I fell in love. I fell in love with the art and music of the coffee. But more important, I fell in love with the people. Your endless dedication to each other and the people you serve are an example for all to follow. You make the world better every day through being of service to others in all the little ways that don't show up on the front pages, but that really matter. Thank you for the bringing the dream to life.

Through The CUP (Caring Unites Partners) Fund, I dedicate half my net proceeds of this book to the Starbucks people. The CUP Fund, through voluntary payroll deductions and fundraisers, provides financial relief to partners facing emergency situations that affect their economic quality of life. The other half of the proceeds will go to the Robert Greenleaf Center for Servant Leadership. Although I never met Robert Greenleaf, his little orange pamphlet made a powerful imprint on my development as a leader, and the center he founded continues to seed the belief in the power and necessity of servant leadership among our current and future leaders.

Endnotes

Introduction

4 At Starbucks there's a little green booklet: The creation of *The Green Apron Book* was spearheaded by Jennifer Ames Karreman, the manager of customer care for North America.

Chapter I

12 Edward de Bono . . . discussed: Edward De Bono, *Six Thinking Hats* (Boston: Little, Brown, 1985; New York: Back Bay Books, 1999).

19 Jim Collins, coauthor of *Built to Last:* James C. Collins and Jerry I. Porras, *Built to Last: Successful Habits of Visionary Companies* (New York: HarperCollins, 1994; Collins Business Essentials, 1997, 2002) chapter 5, pp. 91–114.

The Servant Leader, by James Autry, (New York: Three Rivers Press, 2001), contains a useful discussion of the Purpose, Mission, Values exercises that can be so helpful, but also so misguided if they do not tap into the truth of an organization.

24 Values over Money: Howard Schultz and Dori Jones Yang, *Pour Your Heart Into It* (New York: Hyperion, 1997). This book tells the story of how Schultz built the company "one cup at a time."

26–27 Max De Pree, the legendary head: Max De Pree, *Leadership Is an Art* (New York: Currency Doubleday, 1989, 2004), p. 143.

ENDNOTES

Chapter 2

38 Ken Keyes told this story: Ken Keyes Jr., *The Hundredth Monkey* (Kentucky: Ken Keyes Jr., Devorss, 1981, 1984). For more about this story and research see "Hundreth Monkey Effect" at Wikipedia.com and "The Hundreth Monkey Revisited" in *In Context: A Quarterly of Humane Sustainable Culture* (www.context.org).

39 can't wait for someone's approval: A wonderful parallel concept is developed in a chapter called "Give Yourself an A" in Rosamund Stone Zander and Benjamin Zander's *The Art of Possibility* (Cambridge, MA: Harvard Business School Press, 2000; Penguin Books, 2002).

40 I agree with the description: James C. Collins and Jerry I. Porras, *Built to Last: Successful Habits of Visionary Companies* (New York: HarperCollins, 1994; Collins Business Essentials, 1997, 2002), p. 9.

Chapter 3

60 "providing freedom": Robert Spector and Patrick D. McCarthy, *The Nordstrom Way* (New York: Wiley, 1995), p. 23.

Chapter 5

79 Joseph Campbell used to call this epiphany an *aesthetic arrest:* Campbell was a lifelong scholar of James Joyce, and the concept was taken from the aesthetic definition of art Joyce laid down in *A Portrait of the Artist as a Young Man.*

82 Jerry Manuel: Ben Shpigel, "Mets Coach Would Rather Be Heard Than Seen," *New York Times*, February 24, 2007.

84 Deborah Tannen's work: Deborah Tannen, *You're Wearing That? Understanding Mothers and Daughters in Conversation* (New York: Random House, 2006).

91 former CEO: Alan Murray, "Executive's Fatal Flaw: Failing to Understand New Demands on CEOs," *Wall Street Journal,* January 4, 2007, on Bob Nardelli's departure.

Chapter 7

120 blowout . . . hit: Ray Charles, *Genius Loves Company* (Concord Records/Hear Music, 2004).

120–21 boy soldier in Sierra Leone: Ishmael Beah, *A Long Way Gone* (New York: Farrar, Straus and Giroux, 2007).

Chapter 8

129 Laurence Boldt, the career-planning expert: Laurence G. Boldt, *How to Find the Work You Love* (New York: Penguin/Compass, 1996, 2004), p. 30.

Chapter 9

141 a little orange pamphlet: Robert Greenleaf, *The Servant Leader* (Indianapolis: The Robert K. Greenleaf Center, 1991). Originally published in 1970 by Robert K. Greenleaf, this essay is also available as the first chapter of *Servant Leadership: A Journey into the Nature of Legitimate Power & Greatness* (Mahwah, NJ: Paulist Press, 2002).

154 Organizations that focus on the *performance cycle:* The concept of companion performance cycles and culture cycles is based on the work of The Effectiveness Institute and was developed by Dave Olsen for the Starbucks leadership retreats called Leading from the Heart.

Index

Accountability, 99–112
    erosion, example of, 104–5
    and expectations, 135
    sustainable trade issue, 107
    See also Truthfulness
Action orientation
    action/thought, balance of,
        123–25, 142
    wise action, 122–23
    See also Persistence
Aesthetic arrest, 79
Alling, Jim, 34–35
Alou, Felipe, 82
Apollo, 123
Assertiveness, 57
Automation, positive impact of,
    35–36

Balance
    action/thought, balance of,
        123–25
    and living, 23–24
    and risk taking, 128
Balloons, as symbol of
    recognition, 39–40
Beah, Ishmael, 120–21

Behar, Howard
    begins at Starbucks, 3, 31–32,
        45–46
    career path of, 13–14,
        43–45
    fit with Starbucks, 45–47, 80
    Golden Rule of, 161
    initial impressions of
        Starbucks, 32, 80
    lessons/learning channels for,
        8, 44–45
    one hat, learning about,
        12–14, 58–59
    people orientation of, 16–17,
        45–46
    quotes, collection of, 7–8, 39
    senior leaders, orientation
        of, 62
    as Starbucks North America
        president, 57–59
Behavior change, Hundredth
    Monkey example, 37–38
Big Hairy Audacious Goal
    (BHAG), 19–21
Blanchard, Ken, 13, 107, 151
Bonuses, raising fund for, 105

Books, 120–21
Bottled drinks, 118–19
Built to Last (Collins), 19, 40–41
Burke, James, 132
Buscaglia, Leo, 153

Campbell, Joseph, 79
Canada
    independent thinking example, 59–60
    Toronto lease conflict, 53–54
Cards, birthday/anniversary, 77
Caring, 65–78
    balloon custom, 76–77
    big lover leaders, 140–42
    care, indicators of, 66–67, 69
    and compassionate emptiness, 84–85
    and crisis situations, 131–32
    leader actions related to, 72–75
    leadership team, 74–75
    negative view of, 67–68
    praise, positive effects, 39–40
    relationship to trust, 71, 73
Carpal tunnel syndrome, 35
Chantico, 123
Charles, Ray, 120
Cigarette smoking
    Japan Starbucks, 148–49
    no-smoking policy, 149
Coffee tasting, team meetings, 33
Collins, Jim, 19, 40–41
Communication with heart, 79–97
    compassionate emptiness, 83–91

drink flavors, discussing, 95–96
    feedback as, 90
    language/words, importance of, 102–3
    leader get-togethers, 74–75
    making time for, 90–91
    mother/daughter, 84
    open communication, encouraging, 87–91
    and Open Forums, 94–96
    safety, creating, 89–90
    technology as barrier, 86
    and truthfulness, 99–102
    T-shirt Fridays example, 94
    unspoken, awareness of, 80–83, 91
    See also Listening
Compassionate emptiness, 83–91
    elements of, 85–91
    focus of, 85–86
    See also Communication with heart; Listening
Competition, versus common goals, 34
Consensus, decision making by, 105–6
Crisis, 127–38
    and decision making, 128–29
    management, elements of, 134–37
    and owning truth, 129
    truthfulness, importance of, 132–33

Tylenol crisis, 132
values and strength, 137
Washington, D.C. shootings, 130–32
Culture cycle, 154
Customers
  letters to company, review of, 33, 69–70
  participation in meetings, 70–71
  requests, dealing with, 160–61
  unsatisfied, remaking drinks for, 56

de Bono, Edward, 12
Decision making
  by consensus, 105–6
  and crisis/stress, 128–29
  group conflicts, 106
  and listening, 96–97
  mistakes, ownership of, 109
  and Open Forums, 95–96
Dell, Michael, 90
De Pree, Max, 26–27
Dionysus, 123
Donald, Jim, 35–36
Drinks
  automation, use of, 35–36
  bottled beverages, 118–19
  customer requests, 160–61
  customized, 161–62
  new flavors, discussing, 95–96

Ehrmann, Max, 162
Emotions
  aesthetic arrest, 79

goals, connecting to, 21–22
  passion, Starbucks people, 40
  passion versus professionalism, 14–15
  thought/action balance, 142
Empowerment
  and independent thinking, 55–56, 60–61
  rules, negative impact on, 50–52
Enron, 133
Espresso machines, semiautomated, 35–36
Ethical organization, and truthfulness, 99–102, 132–33
Expectations, and accountability, 135

Failure/mistakes
  celebration of, 119
  drinks, examples of, 118, 123
  fear of, 119
  and job-person lack of fit, 117
  ownership of, 109, 129, 135
Fear(s)
  of failure, 119
  of following dreams, 17–18
  of speaking out, 89–90
  truth as liberator, 110–11
Feedback
  communication as, 90
  See also Praise/recognition
Filters
  functions of, 58
  pros/cons of, 58–59

Financial expansion
  and automated equipment,
    35–36
  bottled drinks, 118–19
  earnings growth, consistency
    of, 20
  food business, 116–17
  labor versus business costs, 35
  licensing business, 142
  music/CDs, 119–20
  new initiatives and filters, 58
  number of openings (2007),
    121
  100 in 3 campaign, 34–36
  overseas. *See* International
    expansion
  Pepsi partnership, 114
  Starbucks North America, 57
  team approach, 33–36
Finn, Charles C., 87
Flow, 91
Food business, 116–17
  development of, 116, 161
  weakness of, 116–17
Ford, Henry, 118
Frappuccino, bottled, 118–19

Gandhi, Mahatma, 82
Geneen, Harold, 100, 115
Genius Loves Company, 120
Goals
  Big Hairy Audacious Goal
    (BHAG), 19–21
  common goals, power of,
    32–36, 40–41
  emotional connection to,
    21–22

  financial targets, meeting,
    33–36
  following, fear of, 17–18
  leadership goal setting, 74–75
  target, path toward, 133–34
Goldstein, Joseph, 84
Green Apron Book, The, 4–7
  principles of. *See* Starbucks,
    guiding principles
Greenleaf, Robert K., 29, 141
Guidelines, versus rules, 51

Herman Miller, 27
Hillel, Rabbi, 72
Hundredth Monkey, 37–38

Independent thinking, 53–63
  assertiveness, 57
  and empowerment, 55–56,
    60–61
  and local leaders, 53–54, 59–60
  positive impact of, 54–55
  right job, indicators of, 61–62
  versus rules, 50–52, 59–60
  and trust in self, 56–59
Innovation, mistakes as, 115
International expansion
  Canada, 59–60, 60
  culture, adapting to, 148–49
  Japan, 148–49
  transfers, resistance to, 41–42

James, William, 11, 17, 114
Japan, smoking issue, 148–49
Job-person fit, 36–47
  and independent thinking,
    60–62

leaving job, Starbucks
examples, 42–43
negative situations, 30–31,
36–37, 42–43, 117
and sense of purpose, 30, 36
Starbucks mission, 40–43,
45–47
and values, 39–40, 44–45
Johnson, Spencer, 13, 107, 151
Jones, Timothy, 119

Kennedy, Robert F., 157
King, Martin Luther, Jr., 82
Kroc, Ray, 99, 111

Layoffs, truthful handling of,
101–2
Leaders/leadership, 139–56
big lover leaders, 140–42
caring, actions related to,
72–75
compensation issue, 149–50
cowboy-style, 140
extreme attitudes toward,
145–47
goal setting by, 74–75
independent thinking, local
leaders, 53–54, 59–60
quiet, power of, 141–44
responsibilities of, 147–52
servant leader, 141–42, 145,
155
understanding people,
complexity of, 153–54
Learning
and listening, 85–86, 88, 96–97
and self-knowledge, 2, 26–27

Leviticus, 113
Leyland, Jim, 82
Licensing business, 142
Listening
compassionate emptiness,
83–91
lack of, negative impact of,
91–94
and learning, 85–86, 88,
96–97
silence, power of, 87
Local management,
independent thinkers,
53–54, 59–60
Long Way Gone, A (Beah),
120–21

McKnight, William, 115
Mandela, Nelson, 110
Manuel, Jerry, 82–83
Mazagran, 118
Merchandising
expansion of, 33–34
function of, 33
Mistakes. See Failure/mistakes
Moore, Colin, 60
Morris, Roly, 54
Music/CDs
development of, 119–20
and Starbucks experience,
114, 120

Negativity
letting go of. See Positive
outlook
and rules, 159
Nordstrom, Bruce, 60–61

Olsen, Dave, 108, 153

One-hat metaphor. *See* Self-knowledge

100 in 3 campaign, 34–36

One Minute Manager, The (Blanchard and Johnson), 13, 107, 151

Open Forums, 94–96

Opportunities, as self-creation, 27–28

Organizational chart, Starbucks, 145

Partners, Starbucks employees as, 102–3

People orientation
  barriers to, 30–32
  of Behar (Howard), 16–17, 45–46
  "best company to work for," 20
  and Big Hairy Audacious Goal (BHAG), 19–21
  common goals, power of, 32–36, 40–41
  guidelines versus rules, 50–52
  Hundredth Monkey example, 37–38
  and individuals, AIDS patient example, 136–37
  necessity for growth, 2, 13, 49, 53
  praise, positive effects, 39–40
  professional development, 150–51
  in salary structure, 24–26

team meetings, 32–36
  versus me orientation, 32–39

Pepsi-Starbucks partnership, 114, 118–19

Performance cycle, 154

Persistence, 113–25
  action, wise, 122–23
  action/thought, balance of, 123–25
  and job-person fit, 117–18
  letting go, time for, 123
  and patience, 121–22
  and products, development of, 116–21
  of Schultz (Howard), 113–14
  target, path toward, 133–34

Piercy, Marge, 52

Political arena, cowboy-style leadership, 140

Positive outlook, 157–65
  benefits of, 162
  customer requests, handling of, 160–61
  importance of, 163–64
  negativity, letting go of, 158–60, 163

Post-It Notes, 115

Praise/recognition
  balloon custom, 76–77
  birthday/anniversary cards, 77
  positive effects of, 39–40

Products, 116–21
  books, 120–21
  bottled drinks, 118–19
  music/CDs, 119–20

Professional development, leader encouragement of, 150–51

Recognition. *See* Praise/ recognition

Relationship conflict, and group decision making, 106

Risk taking
comfort zone, avoiding, 128
and success, 40

Roebling, Mary, 18

Roosevelt, Eleanor, 84

Rules
and controlling people, 61
and disempowerment, 50–52
versus guidelines, 51
versus independent thinking, 50–52, 59–60
and negativity, 159

Safe communication, creating, 89–90

Schultz, Howard
on actions/values match, 143
automated equipment, view of, 35
on cigarette smoking, 148–49
"get big, stay small" concept, 76
hires Behar, 45–46, 80
persistence of, 113–14
vision of, 25, 73–74
and Washington, D.C. shootings, 131

Schumacher, E. F., 76

Self-knowledge, 11–28
and balance, 23–24
goals/dreams, following, 17–18, 21–22

and independent thinking, 56–59
and learning, 2, 26–27
one-hat metaphor, 12–16, 59
opportunities, creating for self, 27–28
positive effects of, 11–13, 27–28
and self-actualization, 17
self-test, 23
self-truth, 109–11
trust in self, 56–57
and values, 22–26

Servant as Leader, The (Greenleaf), 141

Servant leader, 141–42, 145, 155

Silence
and listening, 87
at Open Forums, 95

Six Hat Thinking (de Bono), 12

Small Is Beautiful: Economics as if People Mattered (Schumacher), 76–77

Smith, Orin, 74

Sneed, Richard J., 76

Starbucks
crisis, time of, 130–32
growth. *See* Financial expansion; International expansion
organizational chart, 145
as people-centered company. *See* People orientation
principles. *See* Starbucks, guiding principles
words/terms used by, 102–3

Starbucks, guiding principles
  accountability/truthfulness, 6,
      99–112
  caring, demonstration of, 6,
      65–78
  communication with heart, 6,
      79–97
  crisis, dealing with, 6,
      127–38
  independent thinking, 5,
      53–63
  job-person fit, 5, 36–47
  on leaders/leadership, 7,
      139–56
  persistence, 6, 113–25
  positive outlook, 7, 157–65
  self-knowledge, 5, 11–28
Stress, and life decisions,
      128–29
Support centers, 103
Sustainable trade, 107

Tannen, Deborah, 84
Task conflict, and group
      decision making, 106
Team approach
  alignment, gaining from, 91
  coffee tasting, 33
  consensus and decision
      making, 105–6
  customer letters, review of, 33
  customer participation, 70–71
  filters, 58–59
  leader get-togethers, 74–75
  Open Forums, 94–96
Team approach, tactical decision
      making, 32–36
Terkel, Studs, 49, 52

Thousand Trails, 43
3M, 114–15
Thurman, Howard, 159
Toronto, leasing conflict, 53–54
Torrenga, Dean, 130
Training, outcomes-based,
      51–52
Trust
  relationship to caring, 71, 73
  in self, and independent
      thinking, 56–59
  and truthfulness, 102
Truthfulness, 99–112
  and accountability, 99–102,
      104–5
  corporations, basis of,
      108–9, 133
  and crisis situations, 132–33
  half-truths, 104–5
  and liberation from fear,
      110–11
  owning truth, 109, 129, 135
  self-truth, 109–11
  transparency, importance of,
      107–8
T-shirt Fridays, 94
Tylenol crisis, 132

Values, 22–26
  action/values match, 143
  altered by success, 135–36
  versus financial gain, 24–26
  and inner strength, 137
  and job-person fit, 39,
      44–45
  keeping intact, 22–24
  truth telling. See Truthfulness
Visionary companies, 41

Wager, Deidra, 75
Wages
    leader compensation, 149–50
    Starbucks, 24–26
Washington, D.C. shootings,
    130–32

Watson, Thomas, Jr., 19
Wiesel, Elie, 56
Winfrey, Oprah, 120

You're Wearing That?
    (Tannen), 84